velocit

How can you succeed wh— the only
certainty is change?

Velocity presents seven new laws for businesses and
individuals in a world that is dominated by rapid
change and digital technology.

Written as a conversation between the authors – Ajaz
Ahmed, from AKQA, and Stefan Olander, from Nike
– *Velocity* identifies seven key truths that individuals
and businesses should adopt to thrive. Fast paced,
useful, provocative and highly motivating, *Velocity* will
arm you with actionable ideas to define your future.

With an introduction by Sir Richard Branson.

Ajaz Ahmed is founder of legendary innovation
agency AKQA. Stefan Olander is Vice President of
Digital Sport at Nike. They have worked together
for over twelve years.

www.velocitylaws.com
www.eburypublishing.co.uk

velocity.

THE SEVEN NEW LAWS FOR A WORLD GONE DIGITAL

Ajaz Ahmed *&* Stefan Olander

With an introduction by
Sir Richard Branson

Vermilion
LONDON

5 7 9 10 8 6 4 2

Published in 2012 by Vermilion, an imprint of Ebury Publishing
A Random House Group company

Copyright © Ajaz Ahmed & Stefan Olander 2012

Ajaz Ahmed & Stefan Olander have asserted their right to be identified
as the authors of this Work in accordance with the Copyright, Designs
and Patents Act 1988

The Random House Group Limited Reg. No. 954009

Addresses for companies within the Random House Group can be found at
www.randomhouse.co.uk

The Random House Group Limited supports The Forest Stewardship
Council (FSC®), the leading international forest certification organisation.
Our books carrying the FSC label are printed on FSC® certified paper. FSC
is the only forest certification scheme endorsed by the leading environmental
organisations, including Greenpeace. Our paper procurement policy can be
found at www.randomhouse.co.uk/environment

Printed and bound by CPI Group (UK) Ltd, Croydon, CR0 4YY

ISBN 9780091947569

To buy books by your favourite authors and register for offers visit
www.randomhouse.co.uk.

Contents

From Ajaz

To my parents Khowaj and Sughran, whose kindness, humanity and faith gave my meandering life direction.

From Stefan

To my wonderful, understanding and patient family – Cathrine, Alex, Melina and Lucas. And my wonderful mom, Barbara, for always being there. Jag älskar er.

Introduction by Sir Richard Branson

Virgin is called Virgin because we were new to business and a little bit nervous, but we were also very excited to get started.

The transformation taking place in the world right now makes virgins of us all, and that's the reason why *Velocity* matters. We're living through a time of big and little changes in the way we do just about everything and the only people and organisations guaranteed to make fools of themselves are the ones who think they have got it all figured out.

Change is often seen as a threat, but to an entrepreneur it's oxygen. It's what being alive and enthusiastic about business rests on. When the established ways of doing things are in turmoil, new energy has the best chance to step in and succeed by doing things better than they've always been done before.

A good idea for a business can also become a bad one if your timing is off. (If I had started taking bookings for passenger space flights when I started out in business in 1966, I probably would have been institutionalised.)

When Ajaz founded AKQA in the 1990s, many people thought 'digital' was just a new fad. At Virgin we saw it as exciting. Virgin was one of AKQA's first clients. It's a very natural fit for us to hire a youthful start-up rather than a bureaucratic conglomerate.

Stefan Olander, VP of Digital Sport from Nike, and Ajaz, now chairman of the world's largest digital agency, have put what they've learned on their journey so far in this book to pass it on to anybody not satisfied with the same old routine.

Entrepreneurialism isn't about what happened last night, but about the morning after. If you hide under the covers because you can't face another day of the same old grind, you clearly need more change in your life. If you leap out of bed precisely because, today, everything is going to be different and something is sure to surprise you, then you're halfway there already. This is Velocity. Enjoy the ride.

The Velocity Principles

We don't take it for granted that we're lucky to work with people and companies we love, having careers that feel more like an adventure than a job. Or that the organisations we work for are still thriving in highly competitive and unpredictable times.

We don't take it for granted, either, that we're often asked to share insights, stories and thoughts about how to improve and evolve in a business environment undergoing unprecedented change.

We've had the good fortune to live the digital revolution from the inside, discovering what works and what doesn't. As a result, our work has always obliged us to see 'the new' as an opportunity, never a threat. That's the philosophy, the gift given to us, we want to pass on to you.

Yes, the economic balance of power is shifting to emerging markets. Yes, fearless innovators are reconfiguring the commercial landscape, endangering long-established ways of working. And yes, it's a demonstrable fact that more new technologies, new competitors and impenetrable new bits of jargon appear every day. But what matters is the extraordinary potential amidst all this.

Two billion people are already online. E-commerce sales are $8 trillion a year. Today, change is happening at a pace and scale with no historical precedent.

One of us started his company in London in 1995, aged twenty-one. It's now a global concern with over 1,000 employees, the largest, most awarded firm in its sector. The other joined an iconic brand just as it made early steps into the digital world, leaving the Austrian Alps behind for a journey from Sweden, via The Netherlands, ending up in Oregon. We've lived very different lives and had very different experiences, but, since we first worked together, we've each come to see that our insights, observations and enthusiasm about digital are mirrored in the other.

We started work on this book as a side project about two years ago, recording some of our conversations. We then refined our themes and finally distilled our insights into seven timeless laws that we passionately believe in.

Our intention is to provide some clarity to navigate and define the new environment – an environment we call *Velocity* because of the abilities it requires you to master:

Speed: *because in competitive markets that are being redefined you have to think ahead, but also act fast.*

Direction: *because in uncertain times you can't meander. You need a clear sense of where you're heading, the metrics that matter, the agility and focus to get there.*

Acceleration: *take advantage of speed and direction and you will increase the rate at which you set your work apart, multiplying your contribution.*

Discipline: *because through consistent behaviour you must inspire a culture of strong values, learning, delivery and service. Or nothing will ever get done.*

Velocity is also about optimism. It's a positive force that gives you the mind-set and tools to create a better future.

Not how to do, but what to do

We know a lot of books get bought but fewer get read. So we want to find an accessible way to share what we've learned. To our knowledge, this is the first time a client and agency have teamed up on one.

This is also the first management book that's been written as a conversation. We chose this format because a conversation is the truest way to reflect how we work, think and solve problems. It's the to-ing and fro-ing by which we hone, revise and road-test thoughts. It also means you can dip in and dip out of chapters at will or share any quote you are inspired by or take issue with. The most boring exchanges are the ones where everyone agrees, so we hope you'll want to join in.

Like any book, *Velocity* also captures a moment in time. We don't expect, or claim, to have covered it all. We do hope to spark your curiosity enough to propel you off on your own voyage of discovery – and if you find anything the book missed, we'd love to hear about it.

The future inspires us. We work to inspire

We think the best way to contribute to the future is by giving our all to the present. This book is part of that contribution. We've always been doers and are happiest when we're trying to create something. You lose yourself in something bigger when you've got a goal.

Now it's in your hands and we're back at work, creating what's next. We hope those creations are as satisfying for the people who make them as they are for those who ultimately use them. By sharing our thoughts in *Velocity* we are passing the baton on to you, to do the same. We hope that these principles, laws, stories, insights and behaviours will encourage you to find your own direction.

Ajaz Ahmed & Stefan Olander

The Seven Laws
of Velocity

I. A Smith & Wesson beats four aces

Velocity doesn't care who you are or how good you were yesterday. It's coming for you anyway. Don't be a sitting duck. See the big picture. Find the pain points, see patterns taking shape and act.

Evolve immediately. Entitlement kills.

II. It's easier done than said

Velocity takes courage, focus and determination, but gives back efficiency and rewards intuition, iteration and gutsiness.

Get going. Then get better.

III. The best advertising isn't advertising

Wondering which half of your ad spend is wasted? Velocity says: 'Wrong question. Try again.' Instead of interrupting people, serve them and make them feel something. Sorry, but that takes longer than thirty seconds.

Make meaningful connections.

IV. Convenient is the enemy of right

Velocity needs you to be streamlined. The requisite craftsmanship takes perseverance and discipline. Obsess over important details, and edit ferociously.

Never have anything to apologise for.

V. Respect human nature

Digital is the means, not the end. Technology sometimes obscures this ultimate truth, and makes it easy to forget that at the far side of an app, a Tweet, an anything, there's a person.

Make yourself proud by making people's lives easier, richer and more fun. Don't just give people choice, help them to choose.

VI. No good joke survives a committee of six

For organisations with structures that sand down all rough edges and desiccate anything juicy, something terrible will happen: nothing. It's time for decision-making regimes that hold up to Velocity.

Have the balls to make the calls.

VII. Have a purpose larger than yourself

Velocity will disproportionately reward organisations and individuals that aim to make a meaningful and enduring contribution. Let your imagination and curiosity power progress.

Do the right thing: always play from your heart.

Velocity doesn't care who you are or how good you were yesterday. It's coming for you anyway. Don't be a sitting duck. See the big picture. Find the pain points, see patterns taking shape and act.

Evolve immediately. Entitlement kills.

Stefan: 'Canada Bill' Jones.

Ajaz: That's the man.

Stefan: As a legendary cardsharp in the Old West he knew that the best hand, the best odds and even the house rules all count for nothing if an outsider comes into town with a loaded gun. The gun, a piece of technology, changes every-thing. The guy who thought he was the winner five minutes ago just wants to get out alive now. When someone who sees it completely differently enters the equation, all bets are off.

Ajaz: 'A Smith & Wesson beats four aces.'

Stefan: Whatever conventions and assumptions prevailed before the gunslinger came through the saloon doors with a revolver in hand are now about as useful as a bottle of mineral water would have been to Billy the Kid.

Ajaz: Velocity is changing the business environment as fast as the gunslinger, and we need a bit of Canada Bill's clarity here. When something colossal is happening, like it is now, just trying to protect what you've got is a mistake. A sense of entitlement kills. It is the enemy of innovation.

Stefan: Take the music industry, for instance. Its decline set a pattern for what has happened to many other giant twentieth-century industries too, because it thought it held all the aces. But when file sharing and MP3s came along – once consumers felt the instant gratification of getting songs for free from wherever they are – everything changed. People got hooked on the immediacy and freedom of the digital delivery of music.

At first, it was emotional rather than practical, because sucking down murky tunes at 56k on a dial-up modem might have been exciting due to the novelty, but it lacked a little something ...

Ajaz: ... usually the last twenty-eight seconds of the song.

Stefan: But the technology got better, and as the consumer experience of digital music improved, our need for CDs just evaporated. The music industry cried foul, saying it was stealing. Which it was – although comparing it to shoplifting and trying to guilt-trip people into going back to being good little CD buyers again was a terrible idea. But it was fixated on this. The industry believed the court system could trump the technology, but, even if it was right, legally it was like pushing water up a hill.

The music industry's refusal to see both the threat and the opportunity of digital was more wilful than it was innocent. It couldn't fathom how anything could disrupt the pattern. Or imagine the experience could actually be better for the customer.

Ajaz: What if the music industry had, instead of attempting to end the anarchy, tried to monetise it? What if it had used the millions it spent on lawyers to innovate its way out of the dilemma? What if it created new models to get over what they perceived to be the hindrance of technological change? What if it had understood that audiences want all their music to be portable and they love to share it? What if they made a fair deal with audiences, so it was faster, better quality and more attractive to pay than to pirate? What if you could spend more on the tunes you like and less for music you don't?

Stefan: Those 'what ifs ...?' Now, they're a dime a dozen. What if Kodak or Polaroid had switched gears faster into digital photography? What if Borders had been inspired by Amazon to reinvent their business? What if Blockbuster had created Netflix? What if Sony could match the speed and manufacturing prowess of Samsung, or the category-defining innovation of Apple, aligning hardware, software, content and distribution?

Ajaz: The Borders comparison with Amazon is a reminder of how important data has been to the Velocity revolution, and how few companies noticed in time. In 2001, as their online store struggled and was therefore viewed as a distraction from the core bricks and mortar retail business, Borders made the decision to outsource their e-commerce to Amazon.

Short term, it was convenient. Amazon would manage the transactions, fulfilment and all the perceived complexity that comes with it, while Borders could sit back and take an easy cut. Long term, it was fatal, as Borders never took the necessary steps to transform the organisation so that digital would become a true core competence of their business.

Stefan: Borders' physical locations had significant footfall at the time and e-commerce sales were in their infancy. They may have viewed the tech-heavy online world as something someone else could take off their plate. But in giving up the online piece they gave up the one thing that really matters: *consumer connection*. Every transaction on Amazon's platform was a data point they instead analysed, refined and used to return more value to the consumer. The Amazon experience evolved to provide more choice and convenience than any traditional Borders' retail experience. Ultimately

Without a
platform to
manage and
nurture every
interaction with
its consumer,
a company has
no spine.

Borders had no way of competing at this level of person-alised service.

Ajaz: In 2007 Borders decided to take back the online business, but by then the customer train had already left the station. People got what they needed and more from Amazon. In 2011, Borders filed for bankruptcy.

Stefan: Some businesses claim they're not 'technology companies' and use that as an excuse to shy away from investment and organisational change. Not everyone should strive to become a tech company, but every company should strive to become a technology-proficient organisation, with infrastructure and competencies to manage consumer connections. That doesn't mean beefing up the IT department for its own sake. It's about rethinking the business with the consumer at the centre and then aligning technology, analytics and organisational investments to support it. Without a platform to manage and nurture every interaction with its consumer, a company has no spine.

Ajaz: Organisations should not outsource what should be core competencies. Beneficial use of data is a major contributor to what powers a majority of successful ventures today. The word *data* is the plural of '*datum*' from the Latin 'dare' (which means 'to give'). By contrast, many organisations view data as something you *take*. If they were to view data as something *entrusted* to them by people to refine and return something better, we'd see much stronger value creation for both sides.

Stefan: It's crazy that companies still resist this obvious fact, because brands can't hide any more. We're now in an age of near-perfect information where people have instant access to knowledge about all products at all times, and are empowered to make the best decision for them. The individual's megaphone is massive as well as instant and a single Tweet can start a storm that overpowers the most polished marketing campaign. The enormous upside is that things we love get amplified the same way.

We have a level of transparency that makes it impossible for businesses to hide behind advertising or commercial messages. Practically speaking, we are at the point where a person can stand in a shop and use their phone to answer the question: 'Which one of these products is better for me? And where is the cheapest place to buy it now or have it delivered?'

Ajaz: When you arrive in a new city, you can finally see if your taxi driver really is taking you for a ride or giving you the best journey to your destination. You have the optimum, recommended information that's updated as you move, in the palm of your hand. Previously, you would have been a stranger in a new city with, at best, an out of date guide-book. Now you can have the exchange rate, the language, a live translation of street signs, the best route and the local expertise of thousands in your hands. To embrace Velocity, more businesses need to use data to equip and empower themselves the way their customers already are.

Stefan: With Google indexing civilisation's information and Facebook aggregating all our social connections, it's like 'ask the audience' and 'phone a friend' from *Who Wants To Be A Millionaire?* converging. You get objective data and the opinions of people you trust, anytime, anywhere.

Ajaz: Velocity is a bit like an X-ray machine at the airport. Metaphorically, if you've got stuff in your pockets that shouldn't be there – you'll get found out. If some detail matters to people the way having too big a tube of tooth-paste matters to airport security, it will be detected and you will be taken to task. At the same time, as with flying there's no room for excess baggage or superfluous weight. You need to be agile.

Have you heard of Satchel Paige, the baseball player? He was known for pitching a baseball harder than anyone else back in the day, but he didn't take that superiority for granted. Anything but. In his biography he wrote: *'Don't look back. Something might be gaining on you.'*

Stefan: He clearly understood Velocity and it sounds a lot like Nike. We're often asked how we're able to stay ahead. People seem to want one magic explanation: is it our products, people, endorsements or marketing? All those play their part, but actually the true driver behind it all is the *athlete*. It's the unforgiving demands of the world's finest athletes that drive us.

Ajaz: Does that mean we need to be superhuman with perfect bodies and extraordinary intellects to match? If it does, I haven't a hope.

Stefan: Not at all. It's more about the ethos, or spirit of athletes. They push themselves and expect us to do the same.

Ajaz: The athlete's mind-set is useful. Being canny and streetwise. Having the determination to contribute; the desire to improve; the hunger to learn; the slight paranoia that prompts you to think about what might go wrong; the optimism and hard work to make sure it doesn't.

Stefan: It's also about character: the qualities of personality not easily measured, just as much as the ones that are. Like being dependable, having the integrity to keep commitments, being aware of areas that can do with improvement. That last one is a key part of why athletes are such great models for preventing an entitlement culture.

'Don't look back.
Something might
be gaining on you.'

Satchel Paige, legendary baseball pitcher

Ajaz: People always talk about 'confidence' in many sports, but in business it's about being assured without being so over-confident that you stop asking questions. It's really easy to lose it. And the quickest way is believing that you're great. It's not about a job title as a sign of prestige. It's not about how many trophies are stacked up in the cupboard. It's not about glowing media reviews. It is about the responsibility to not settle, especially when you're winning.

Stefan: Nike's first defining moment came when co-founder Bill Bowerman, a genius, track-obsessed coach, used a waffle iron to innovate a lighter running shoe. Ever since then, we've been completely focused on creating the best products to give our athletes the edge. It's the translation of this passion into *everything* we do that makes Nike what it is. We never take any win for granted. The second you think you hold the upper hand you lose your focus.

In a world where 0.01 of a second may be all there is between winning or not, the smallest detail makes all the difference. Obsess the details and the rest will sort itself out.

Ajaz: Ask a great coach, 'How do you win a match?' and you will get the answer, 'Do a hundred things better than anyone else.' People who approach work as an opportunity to learn are more satisfied with their performance and more eager to take on new challenges. They are not trying to prove they're the smartest, but more likely to learn from their own experiences. They perceive tasks as 'challenges' rather than 'problems'.

It's also about seeking and giving feedback. Good coaches combine observation and imagination. They listen and provide regular reaction. In a high-performance team, feedback has to be accurate, specific and well-timed. There isn't room for ambiguity or procrastination when literally every second counts on the pitch.

But in many businesses, feedback is about filling in forms in some time-consuming annual performance review ceremony. It should be about inspiring the best performance at the exact time it can make most impact, rather than linger for days, weeks, even months. If you're still doing things that way, you are by definition missing opportunities and underperforming. Feedback delayed is feedback denied.

Stefan: The best coaches are thoughtful, too, about the language they use to motivate their teams. When an athlete does well, they will praise the individual for the training effort put in or for their contribution on match day, rather than say that they are 'a natural' or 'gifted'. The idea is to guide a player to work at more of what they know will make a tangible difference on the field, rather than believing they are somehow unusual and don't have to keep trying.

Ajaz: They also instil a courageous way of thinking so that their teams aspire to go beyond limits of what may have previously been considered likely or achievable.

Stefan: It's the ability to see what's not there, to think the impossible, to work towards it that matters. Athletes have always known they have to keep progressing. They've always had to contend with the possibility, the inevitability, that some young kid who wants it more and is willing to work for it will soon arrive on the scene with a bag of new tricks, hoping to overtake them.

Ajaz: The things that provide a sense of safety, security and self-esteem today just might not be relevant tomorrow. Somebody else may make a discovery or uncover a new opportunity away from those who keep thinking they know it all.

The very first elite athletes, in ancient Greece, received a wreath of laurel leaves when they won a contest, and, ultimately, the expression 'Don't rest on your laurels' must go right back to that time. They knew that, if you're basking in the afterglow of your last successful race, chances are that someone's already out there training harder than you for the next one.

Stefan: When a person, team or organisation has won some recognition, it's natural to lose some of the hunger that got them to the level of achievement in the first place. For that reason it has to be about both valuing what you've achieved and not taking anything for granted. It's the idea of training like you're number two to remain number one.

Ajaz: Success has the seeds of failure built in. Rarely is there the inclination to mess with a winning formula until it's too late. But it's when you're most successful that you're also most vulnerable. Customer loyalty can be transient, especially in the software, hi-tech and consumer electronics industries. Companies that had dominant share of a market can quickly lose it. They conclude they have the market sewn up and can't conceive their share could be eroded. Once they fall into that trap, the sands can crumble at incredible speed.

When I was fifteen, I got the chance to work for a company called Ashton-Tate. At that time, in their heyday, Ashton-Tate had around 70 per cent market share of the database software market – the precursor to many of the thriving businesses today that store digital information, multimedia and content, making it easily accessible.

As with many Silicon Valley legends, Ashton-Tate grew from a humble start in a garage to become the third largest software company on the planet, behind Microsoft and

Lotus (which was then bought by IBM). The much-anticipated fourth version of its flagship product dBASE launched, but it wasn't ready.

Then, three things happened: Ashton-Tate dramatically lost market share; their stock market value got hammered; and a smaller rival acquired them.

The office rumour at the time was that there was a pivotal meeting between the CEO and his development team. Even though he realised the product was not up to scratch, the CEO told them to ship it because of board pressure to meet the quarterly Wall Street numbers.

Around the same time, Microsoft was launching the Windows graphical user interface to replace its MS-DOS command-line system.

dBASE IV launched and it got bad reviews. Corporate customers who were expecting a powerful new product to meet their evolving needs instead received something bug-ridden.

Ashton-Tate hadn't seen Windows and the graphical user interface as a threat. This was partly because the early versions that people had seen pre-launch were not particularly sophisticated. Seeing the rival's teething problems rather than its potential, Ashton-Tate remained convinced that people would continue to interface with computers by typing in complex commands on a keyboard, not clicking on a screen.

So this double-whammy knocked out Ashton-Tate. There's a tragic irony about launching a product early to keep the share price up, only to see it plummet.

It was a terrible end for Ashton-Tate, nicknamed 'Ashton-Great' by staff when considered top in its field. Now the company lives on only in Wikipedia and distant memories.

Being exposed to all that when I was a teenager means it's something that's forever etched on my mind. To a degree, it keeps me slightly paranoid.

There's another lesson from the Ashton-Tate story that has nothing to do with disruptive innovation. It's about quality control and fixing a problem quickly. First Ashton-Tate released a product that had faults, but, worse, they didn't acknowledge or put right the problem quickly enough. Customers abandoned Ashton-Tate's technology faster than the company fixed the problem.

Stefan: The disruption in various industries is also happening in global economies. It's accentuated and fuelled by technology. Emerging economies and start-ups don't need to dance to anyone else's tune. The map of the

There's never been a better time to be an entrepreneur with a disruptive idea.

world from an economic perspective is starting to see an enormous shift in gravity.

Ajaz: There's going to be a dispersal of economic authority. I don't think there's ever been a better time to be an entrepreneur with a disruptive idea. Relatively low-cost, accessible technology has created fewer barriers to entry. The web, social networks and app stores provide immediate global distribution for the best ideas to spread quickly. This digital infrastructure accelerates the velocity of distribution.

Stefan: There's a new awareness and recognition of the obligation that everything an organisation does needs to be done truthfully and intelligently.

Ajaz: That's ultimately how people are going to evaluate the companies they want to do business with.

Stefan: Otherwise they just get replaced with something else. It's not even that they don't see the opportunities or threats ahead. It's that, when the world changes, they simply respond with more of the same as what worked before. Even worse is that they start to serve the organisation structure, the politics, rather than serve the people who pay the bills.

Ajaz: A friend of mine once worked at an agency called HHCL that I greatly admired. It was probably the most influential agency of its generation, creating one memorable idea after another.

Just when the agency was receiving most recognition through prestigious awards, glowing articles in the press, and was universally considered to be at the very top of its field, it dramatically fell from grace.

It started losing clients. It stopped winning pitches. Then it vanished completely, having been absorbed into a larger holding company and renamed. My friend who worked there told me that when the agency was at the height of its influence, it became inward-looking, instead of focusing on the work and the clients. The motivations within the company had changed. The price this company paid for self-absorption was its disappearance.

Stefan: Sounds like a sense of entitlement led to their downfall?

Ajaz: I found an article in a national newspaper in which one of the agency's founders is quoted:

> *'I think there was a tendency to sit back and not try as hard as we could.'*

In the same article one of their former clients says:

> *'They had not moved on. What was new and different … now feels a bit tired and predictable. There are other agencies smart enough to know they have to reinvent themselves and keep changing.'*

There were also feuds among the partners. Recalling what happened to his agency, another of the founders wrote in his blog:

> *'We let the original dynamic of the partners dissipate. In other words, we fought too much. This came about through politics and envy. It's weird – there were all sorts of personality differences between us, but they got subsumed when we were young and struggling. However, as soon as success came our way, we fought like cat and dog.'*

Stefan: Companies need to remove friction, not add it. The future is about making what we already do much easier. For me, the next decade is about simplifying our lives and solving our everyday needs in a more enriching way. That means a much smarter approach with less 'user interface' and more intelligence.

Ajaz: One of the reasons why it's a struggle for an established organisation to innovate is because the existing team already has its hands full doing the current job. Big organisations are usually built for efficiency, not for innovation. There's a core business to keep running, so every task becomes predictable and repeatable. In many respects, innovation is seen as the opposite of efficiency because it is not routine and has unpredictable outcomes. This can create an environment in which there is no investment into future revenue streams because of the short-term impact on margins. As a result, the established business becomes resistant to innovation because it feels threatened by it, creating forces that actively discourage new thinking.

Stefan: For a company it means embracing innovation as part of the DNA and solidifying the importance of it across the organisation. You have to institutionalise innovation.

Ajaz: Institutionalise innovation? That sounds contradictory but it's the method for firms to embrace rather than feel intimidated by change. What about organisations that have not embedded innovation?

Stefan: It's about creating a dedicated team that's empowered and has separate resources. Most importantly this team should not be isolated – it needs to be connected and integrated into the core business.

Ajaz: The leader's clear mandate is to increase revenues, develop new products and markets, drive profitability and create a sustainable business for the benefit of customers, employees, management, shareholders and the community. The leadership team's role is to grow companies by adding value to generate premium returns. That means leaner organisational structures for quick decision-making and the encouragement of more experimentation.

Stefan: Because innovation, by its nature, is an experiment with unknown outcomes.

Ajaz: There's always risk but good leadership is about taking a calculated, considered risk.

Stefan: There can be painful lessons when experimenting. However, understanding why something did not work, reflecting on it and not repeating the errors – that's progress. The ability to learn will enable better decision-making. Better decision-making and judgement increases profit.

Ajaz: When innovative companies have the advantage of scale combined with an efficient performance engine, shareholders are rewarded. Nike is the most valuable company in its category. Apple is the most valuable company in the world. By contrast, British Telecom has 75 million miles of copper wire in its network. That network is therefore worth around £50 billion: more than three times the company's market capitalisation of around £15 billion. BT's old business is worth more than its new business but shareholders are not getting any credit for it, because it's not just about infrastructure, but contribution. BT reports good numbers each quarter but stock-market analysts want it to innovate more.

Stefan: Without new markets, new customers or new revenue streams, a business can only grow so much. Innovation is about adapting to and benefiting from change that might arise because of new technologies, new customers or new competitors entering the space.

Ajaz: Big companies rarely get excited about opportunities that they perceive as small. It means they don't want the hassle or distraction of something experimental or risky that they perceive will have marginal returns, especially if the established business is doing okay.

The result can be incremental innovation or small improvements to existing products rather than anything radical.

Therefore a start-up will often champion disruptive innovation that changes the rules of the game and makes an existing business model obsolete. But being revolutionary and pioneering on its own isn't enough. It's only when a breakthrough is combined with scale that the organisation can reap advantages.

Stefan: Many businesses are 'institutionally analogue': stuck in structures and logistical straitjackets that had an obvious function and a rational purpose fifty, twenty, even fifteen years ago. But for the past decade that way of doing things has been evaporating.

Ajaz: Sometimes the organisation becomes aware of changes that are affecting its industry, but do not act upon it. In other organisations the ideas are lost in a sea of bureaucracy. In this scenario, when an individual has true resilience, conviction and belief in the idea, they might leave the company to start a new business they passionately believe in. Often, there are fewer barriers to starting a new business than creating one within an established organisation.

We've already seen media that was analogue make the transition to digital. The next stage is that analogue products are becoming smart and connected. It's being called 'the internet of things'. That means every kind of 'thing', from your body to cars to roads, is connected and integrated in a more solutions-oriented way.

Practically it means never losing your keys or, better, not needing keys in the first place. Making an existing behaviour

Innovation,
by its nature,
is an experiment
with unknown
outcomes.

more beneficial for you. For example, weighing scales that give you a snapshot of your health, not just your weight. Providing an early warning instead of waiting for an annual check up or just when you have become ill. Prevention is always better than the cure.

Stefan: New businesses born from the digital world don't have to fight old structures. They can start small but as we've pointed out, the best ideas use the inherent distribution built into a digital infrastructure to spread. They can organise themselves around what matters – the consumer – rather than business segments, sub-brands or divisions. They put analytics at the heart of it all to have a finger on the pulse of users rather than relying on lagging POS data, quarterly tracking studies or focus groups. It's real time or no time. Period.

That's why it makes sense for an established company to act more like a start-up and force disruption. Creating a properly funded internal start-up that has the freedom to live by the Velocity laws, making sure it's got full CEO and senior management support, can be a pretty low-risk opportunity to learn fast what has to change.

Ajaz: California has this incredible ecosystem that breeds one start-up after another. It comprises brilliant educational institutions like Stanford. There's an environment that nurtures entrepreneurship. There's an investor community that act as coaches, putting their money where their mouth is. There is a sense of positivity that must have something to do with the great climate. These cultural, strategic and organisational attributes have led to sustained success and leadership in areas like software, biotech, healthcare, semiconductors and, of course, computing.

Stefan: It's the unique partnership of vision, entrepreneurs, education and equity investment that's one of the reasons Silicon Valley has an unmatched track record for producing businesses that can scale quickly.

Ajaz: Also the willingness to destabilise what you have in order to get what you want. It's a characteristic of an entrepreneur who would rather put their old businesses out of business than have a rival do it for them. But few people are willing to dismantle an existing organisation structure to replace it with something that has yet been proven.

Stefan: When you are taking that important leap into the unknown, you can and must draw confidence from the connection that matters most: a clean, straight line to the customer.

If we ask why whatever product or service we create will make people's lives easier, better or more fun, rather than starting with how it might just contribute to the bottom line, we'd see more successful businesses. Velocity has made this a unique time to take informed risks because in this transition to an interconnected world, where new technology changes the rules every day, nobody has all the answers.

Ajaz: Which is why mastering Velocity is about understanding technology but not worshipping it, and about making the most of the data without becoming enslaved by it. Computers can only tell you so much, and about some of the most important things they can tell you absolutely nothing.

Stefan: The writer Carl Hiaasen, who has spent his life in Florida, wrote a great essay about how, for all the improvements in weather forecasting technology, the ability of meteorologists to specifically, helpfully, predict a hurricane's landfall has basically failed to improve over decades.

He points out that modern satellite pictures now allow us to trace a tropical storm from its very first drop. 'But so what?' Hiaasen asks. 'All we bought ourselves is an extra week of high anxiety.' For all our reams of data, we still don't know any earlier than our ancestors whether the hurricane is coming for us or not. The best we can do is wait, watch and be ready to run. For all the statistics now available to him, Hiaasen says that forty-seven hurricane seasons have taught him that the most useful piece of data you can learn about a hurricane is this: 'all it takes is one'.

Ajaz: Business sometimes feels like a hurricane. So if we're doing Velocity Book Club show and tell, anyone who has read *The Black Swan* by Nassim Taleb can't help but be haunted by the anecdote about the Thanksgiving turkey. Based on everything the turkey knows from experience – historical data, you might say – life on the farm is great. He gets fed each day; he walks around in the sunshine and fresh air. This lifestyle continues, predictably, for several years.

Then one afternoon in the autumn – surprise! A bolt from the blue. Or so it feels. Because, lacking any ability to get outside his context or his frame of reference, the turkey doesn't know he's a sitting duck, as it were.

Stefan: Fortunately, people have bigger brains than turkeys. We can sometimes conceptualise our way out of potential problems that past experience wouldn't, by itself, have taught us enough about.

Ajaz: How can people see approaching danger or opportunity, so they're not blindsided? One way is to keep a wide lens – much wider than might seem necessary. Notice

If we ask why whatever product or service we create will make people's lives easier, better or more fun, rather than starting with how it might contribute to the bottom line, we'd see more successful businesses.

movement in your peripheral vision. Pick up on the weak signals. Overhear conversations. You are what you read. You are what you do. You are what you experience.

Stefan: The smartest people I've met are the ones who have had the most diverse range of experiences. At the heart of innovation is following a path that isn't the same as the mainstream as it provides the ability to make connections that are out of the ordinary.

Ajaz: It helps to spend time learning points of view from outside your industry. Retailers, for example, can learn from the best hotels when it comes to customer service. Creative agencies can learn from the best restaurants who ensure consistent quality in anything that ever leaves the kitchen.

Many companies are what private equity people call 'forever tiny'. In other words, they don't grow. I see it differently. Innovation is our canvas for growth. Growth is the creator of opportunity, the provider of progress.

Sure, it might be *easier* to keep things the way they are, but there are problems with it. You're limiting your contribution to society for potentially enhancing people's lives, to the economy, to job creation. You're cutting yourself off from the future.

Stefan: To have ideas that are radically different requires experiences that are radically different. It's best to diverge from the conventional path as this can help you solve problems in different ways.

Ajaz: Environment and influences make a big difference. I was lucky to grow up in the Thames Valley, which is considered the Silicon Valley of England. In addition to being a beautiful part of the world, it's where many tech firms are located. So while I was a kid, I was conscious of exciting, fast-growing companies, many of which had arrived from California and had this gravitational pull that attracted me.

I feel extremely accountable to the organisations and people I've been influenced by, because otherwise you're pretending it came from nowhere when it didn't.

As a result, it's a goal to ensure every location where AKQA has an office is the most multicultural environment anyone has worked in so that we have a broad range of influences. Having people from so many different places and backgrounds means approaching a challenge from a different point of view and learning something new every day.

Stefan: Be curious. Observe people. Notice changes in their needs and behaviours. Don't get stuck in routines, try something new every day and always fill the well with insights based on your area of interest or responsibility, and hopefully a little beyond it.

I usually start the day with the mobile versions of my Swedish newspaper, *TechCrunch*, the *New York Times* and *Mashable*. In about three hundred seconds I have a pretty good grasp of what happened in technology, sport and world affairs while I was sleeping. Add Twitter and I've got real-time updates on relevant topics throughout the day.

Ajaz: As your daily ritual shows, we rely on an ecosystem of news rather than a single source. It means we get different points of view. It also means that a three-hundred-person newsroom isn't a prerequisite to being a modern media owner.

Stefan: The news playing field has been levelled. Tweets, or posts from individuals on a photo-sharing service like Instagram, can be just as valuable as those from a media brand, especially as they're firsthand testimony from people who are actually there. It's like the student said in the market research group: 'If the news is important, it will find me.'

Ajaz: A service like Flipboard assembles your ecosystem of sources. It combines content from existing titles like *Wired*,

The Economist or *Surfer* magazine; Tweets and photos from people you follow; status updates from family, all put together in an elegant package for your phone or iPad. It means you're not bombarded with facts and data in chronological order, but a more rhythmic and elegant experience. The whole idea or promise of a personalised news channel or 'Daily Me' is here.

Stefan: But it doesn't need to be daily. It's fresh all the time.

Ajaz: Despite all that real-time information, none of us has a clue how the world might change in the next twenty-four hours.

Stefan: There's no forecast in business. You have to put your faith in a vision and then hire the best people you can to build it. You have to be willing to reward anybody who finds smart ways to reduce the friction in your life. You also have to make the most of what you *do* know, which means channelling your ability to reinvent the obvious.

Ajaz: One reason reinventing the obvious is so important is that many things we do, it seems to me, are just long-standing bad habits, like clogging up the roads so we can all be at our jobs between 9am and 6pm on so-called 'weekdays'. It would relieve traffic and commuter congestion on

There's no forecast in business. You have to put your faith in a vision and hire the best people you can.

public transport if millions of people didn't have to be at the office at the same time.

Stefan: There's no reason whatsoever not to do this, other than the fact that we've 'always done it that way'. I'd venture to say that if people logged on from wherever they already were during rush hours instead of getting frustrated in traffic jams, general productivity would increase across the board.

Ajaz: That's not daydreaming. Things don't have to be one way just because they always have been. Have you heard of e-cloths? These are cloths made of microfibres woven at a density of 480,000 strands per centimetre. With tap water alone, they clean up better than any of the solvent-based products under the sink. Chemical-based cleaning products' days are numbered. E-cloths are an example of how intelligent design can cut a whole load of pain-points, economic and environmental, out of the equation at once.

Stefan: So, in conclusion: change is hard, but remaining stuck in your ways is potentially death by a thousand cuts. It's easier to register this fact than it is to do something about it.

Ajaz: I've been lucky to work with more than my fair share of great companies. So I get asked to define what I believe to be the hallmark of the best enterprises. I summarise it in three words: attention to detail.

This isn't just attention to detail for the product, or the customer service, or the operations, logistics, finances or marketing. It's every detail.

A comparison is one I learned from an in-flight documentary about the human genome. On this particular journey, I discovered that DNA has four different chemical building blocks, abbreviated as A, T, C and G, and that in the human genome about three billion base pairs are arranged along the chromosomes in a particular order for each unique individual.

All it takes is four of the chemicals to be out of sequence for serious problems to occur ... four out of three billion.

I think it's the same with organisations. The companies that have exemplary attention to detail, the highest level of quality control across their business and the ability to look ahead are also the ones that endure.

A Smith & Wesson beats four aces

Evolve immediately. Entitlement kills.

Be the disrupter, not the disrupted

No one owes you anything. When you're faced with altered conditions or contexts, rapid acceptance of your new reality combined with appropriate action can help to turn potential disaster into opportunity. Athletes have to be brutally honest about their own strengths and weaknesses to reach the top. Even when they get there, they never think they're too good to be coached or keep learning. Strive for a constant state of responsiveness so you can take Velocity in your stride. Be your own competition.

It's good to be first. It's better to be good.
It's best to be both

It's tempting to believe that the market will obey your will, forgive your compromises and beat a path to your door. It won't. Ensure a high level of quality control across everything you do. Benefit from digital distribution platforms that provide immediate scale which allow good ideas to spread quickly.

You can't improve what you can't measure

Quality and integrity is the driver of earnings and growth. No one ever developed an ability to make better decisions through successes alone. Innovation has unpredictable outcomes. Embrace it and create a culture that celebrates experimentation and learning as much as revenue and profit.

Travel light

Velocity moves fast, and sooner or later exposes everything to public view like an X-ray machine. Don't carry more than you need, or get caught saying one thing when you're doing another – risks that get greater the bigger your firm becomes. Be agile, take only what you need to make your contribution, so you'll be ready to react to new opportunities and not get stuck at check-in with everybody else.

IT'S EASIER

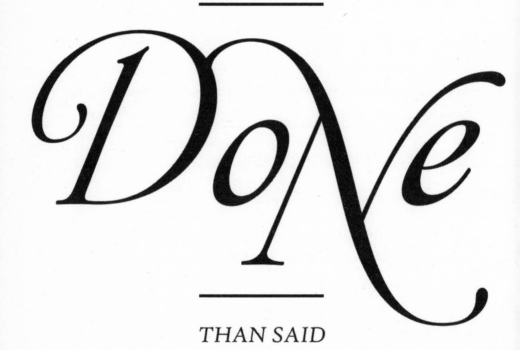

THAN SAID

Velocity takes courage, focus and determination, but gives back efficiency and rewards intuition, iteration and gutsiness.

Get going. Then get better.

Stefan: 'Beta' used to be the preserve of scientists and engineers, a word employed to describe a product in a pre-perfected state. It has crept into everyday vocabulary, and rapid prototyping – or, to use the true technical term, 'getting stuff done fast' – is now the norm in many areas. It takes getting used to, but, done right, it's full of opportunities. In essence, the digital world forces us to spend less time debating the perfect solution in everlasting internal meetings and more time executing the best solution.

Ajaz: It's only 'easier done than said' when the organisation has a culture that's obsessed with consistently delivering. That's the journey a company has to make, consciously going from saying to doing. So the behaviour amplifies the words. There are two kinds of agency: those with offices that look like showrooms and those that look like workshops. The agencies that look like showrooms are too removed from execution. They can't move fast, let alone accelerate. Execution needs to be a natural reflex. An organisation needs more 'doers' who are motivated by making stuff. Nearly every idea still starts with a sketch, but being able to create a working prototype is better.

Stefan: Facebook prototypes stuff all the time. From 2008 to 2010, while growing from one hundred million to five hundred million users, they launched a number of different homepages and made a slew of other changes. What's interesting is how they did it, and how they did not do it. They focused on observing where users spent time and which features were sticky. Based on that, they laid down their best bet, went live with the changes, then sat back and evaluated. They ditched what didn't work and kept refining what did.

They didn't pull together massive focus groups to give them the answer, and they never asked anyone's permission.

Ajaz: They didn't need to. Facebook is taking responsibility for editing and curating the services and designs they believe will be of greatest benefit for users. They have the data and use the service themselves so are also the audience.

Stefan: We quickly learned to like what Facebook was 'forcing' on us. My favourite example was when NewsFeed was first introduced. When it was launched, there was uproar. A lot of people felt too much info was being shared. But how did they register their outrage? Where did they denounce NewsFeed? On NewsFeed itself!

'We don't build services to make money; we make money to build better services.'

Mark Zuckerberg, Facebook

Back in 2007, at a team meeting we had in San Francisco, Mark Zuckerberg said that was when he knew it was going to be a winning feature. Later, he told David Kirkpatrick, author of *The Facebook Effect*, 'Whenever we roll out any major product there's some sort of backlash. We need to be sure we can still aggressively build products that are on the edge and manage this big user base. I'd like us to keep pushing the envelope.'

Facebook Timeline has launched and it's a bold move. To make that big a change to the service is incredibly brave, and I doubt many businesses would have the guts to do that with an installed base of almost a billion users. But then again they have established a position based upon a superb platform of human connectivity unlike anything the world has ever seen. I like what Mark Zuckerberg wrote in his recent letter to prospective investors on Facebook's social mission:

> 'We don't build services to make money; we make money to build better services.'

In the same letter Mark describes Facebook's culture as 'The Hacker Way':

> 'The Hacker Way is an approach to building that involves continuous improvement and iteration. Hackers believe that something can always be better, and that nothing is ever

complete. They just have to go fix it – often in the face
of people who say it's impossible or are content with the
status quo.'

Ajaz: With myriad choices, creating an installed base is a difficult task. Then figuring out how to monetise the service and keep the users engaged once the initial novelty has worn off can be even more challenging. An organisation needs to have a roadmap and the ability to execute ideas immediately. Some call this creating a 'culture of execution'. There's an argument that culture is the by-product of consistent behaviour. It means that if the leaders participate, encourage and reward a particular behaviour then it will get built into the organisation. Leaders should be deeply engaged and reward the ability to execute rather than just talk about an idea. It also means that execution is something that's not beneath anyone. Being focused on quality delivery is one of the most important attributes a leader can have. Maybe charts with fancy buzzwords and the latest management fad have their place, but I'm not sure where that is.

Managers need to focus on tangible outcomes that are making an impact with very real deliverables. They should not get confused into thinking the chart is the deliverable. Just because it's on a chart does not make it true.

Nearly all customer touch points are going digital. So every brand is going to have to become a software company.

When a product or service is being subsidised by the manufacturer or advertising so it's free to the user, we're getting comfortable with 'beta culture'. It started getting broad acceptance with software and services, but with 'the internet of things' and connected products we can now begin to imagine a point where instant consumer feedback can be applied to anything.

It facilitates a different kind of exchange between customer and brand. You give the customer the option of knowingly opting in to your constantly evolving creation, in exchange for the priceless road test that only real users can subject your invention to.

The early-adopting customer opts in to your new system or feature, and in so doing makes an implicit deal with you, the creator. As long as the good new things your product introduces into the customers' lives aren't outweighed or crippled by its kinks, bugs and imperfect initial design choices, they'll stick around, because they get where you're going and feel they've been a part of the journey.

Stefan: Nobody holds it against Thomas Edison that the first thousand light bulbs he designed fizzled out the instant the switch was flipped. But they'd be mad if the one that was supposed to work, which they'd paid the full price for, didn't. So you're probably right. Pretty soon we'll move through version 0.1 through 0.5 through 0.51, asymptotically approaching a final 1.0 but never quite getting there because of all the great input (and bugs) we get along the way.

Ajaz: Asymptote? What's that? Fortunately I have the answer to every question in my hand, so, courtesy of my iPhone. 'Siri, what does asymptote mean?'

Siri: I found this for you ...

Ajaz: Here we are. A page from WolframAlpha. 'An asymptote is a line or curve that approaches a given curve arbitrarily closely.' It has an illustration and a detailed definition if I want that. You were telling me about these guys in Chicago?

Stefan: It's an example of digital making things easier to do than they are to talk about. It was a project posted on Kickstarter, a funding platform for creative ideas, by Scott Wilson and his independent design shop, Minimal. Their idea was to turn the new iPod Nano into a touchscreen wrist watch by converting it using a kit. They designed two models: TikTok, a lower-priced snap-in plastic version, and LunaTik, a more premium aluminium model.

They wanted to raise $15k in a month in order to cover tooling and production costs and hopefully get a small batch of watch kits manufactured. Well, guess what? They raised nearly $80k in the first day alone. Six days later, they'd raised more than $270,000, and when the investment window shut at the end of 30 days they'd banked $942,578 from 13,512 global backers, all of whom effectively pre-ordered the wrist watch kits.

Ajaz: Using the collective cooperation of the general public to raise funds in an accessible way, or 'crowdfunding' as it's being called, allows people with ideas to sidestep traditional avenues of investment. In the past you'd have to produce a proof of concept. Then make a business plan. Then take the plan around in the hope of raising money to make it a reality. Upshot: a good chance of it not happening, with a lot of time and energy down the drain.

Jim Breyer, the venture partner at Accel who sits on the board of Facebook, has said that his company sees ten thousand media business plans a year and they invest in about ten.

Stefan: Internally, we do this at Nike. There is a lot of intuition and 'Hey, what do you think of this?' within the company. When we first developed Nike+ in collaboration with Apple, we couldn't very effectively go out and do a bunch of research, because there wasn't anything like it on the market for anyone to refer to.

They wanted to raise $15k in a month. They raised $80k in the first day.

I especially remember one key meeting between Nike and Apple executives, and a first-hand, eye-opening peek into the genius of Steve Jobs. The teams from both companies had worked for months, preparing a complete deck of how the entire experience was going to be brought to market. An extensive presentation was loaded on to the screen.

We were sitting in Apple's boardroom at their Cupertino headquarters in California all ready to kick off with slide 1 of 164, when Jobs, slowly rocking back and forth in his chair with his feet against the conference table, said:

'Hold on. Before we start getting into details ...

Do we have a product?'

Silence ensued. He continued:

'How accurate is the shoe sensor, and what will we sell it for?'

The engineers replied that the algorithms were being refined and that we couldn't tell exactly how precise it would be, but if runners did a manual calibration we could get it really accurate.

We also hadn't decided how to price it, and, as discussions went back and forth around what margin to go for, Jobs immediately shot back:

'If it's not 90 per cent accurate for 90 per cent of the people, right out of the box, I don't think we have a product. And it shouldn't cost more than $29. We make iPods and you make shoes, so this must be a completely frictionless experience combining the power of the two. Can you get it there? Because if you can't, we might as well adjourn.'

The teams nailed it and together we created a revolutionary experience that would change running forever and define the model for most digital running experiences out there today.

Steve Jobs' and the team's ability to have a crystal-clear understanding of what it takes to create true value for consumers makes all the difference.

Ajaz: Nike knows about sport and athleticism. Apple knows about simplifying and humanising technology. Only by collaborating on how to merge physical and digital in the most elegant way did you create a completely new category.

Stefan: Exactly. Take what's right there in front of you. Tweak it and create a whole new space by making what people already do just a little bit easier. Combining skills and collaboration creates such value for consumers and the enterprise. On the day of its launch in May 2006, both Nike's and Apple's stock prices made a sizeable jump.

But to come back to the launch-learn-relaunch point, for all the amazing competence within these two companies we knew we'd get tons of fresh input from the runners. In the last five years we've grown the ecosystem of Nike+ Running with the Nike+ GPS iPhone app, the Nike+ SportBand and the Nike+ SportWatch GPS.

Many great features on both the service and those products have either been inspired or come straight from our runners, a very passionate and vocal community that has logged over four hundred million miles together. When we put a 'tell us what you think' button up on nikeplus.com, we get 15,000 responses in a day. From people who willingly tell us everything they need. We're especially interested in the things we haven't thought of. There were (and, we've since learned, always are) an impressive number of these.

Even when the feedback is straight-up angry, you still have to be ready to use it – if you don't, you'll pay. Nike+ had server issues, and the online community were incredibly vocal and justifiably unhappy about it. Our Running GM Jayme Martin sent an apology to the entire community and the team personally answered every single comment that came back.

We then focused on making sure the core service was stable, while, in parallel, building a completely new experience from the ground up, largely based upon everything we had learned over the past five years. We've reduced and reduced and reduced so all superfluous features and functionality have been removed and we now have a lean, fast, simple experience with a clean, purpose-driven design.

The original proposition, which went live in 2006, was based on merging traditional running insights with the notion that music can be a powerful motivational tool.

Running is part of Nike's heritage, so concern was voiced by a number of core runners within the company who claimed that running with music wasn't authentic, and that this project would consequently jeopardise our status as a credible running brand and should be stopped. But Mark Parker, our CEO, who himself is a very accomplished runner, wouldn't have it:

> *'Innovation is about embracing change, but understanding context,' he said. 'We'll always make great running shoes. That's authentic. And now we'll offer a new way to get motivated through a system that allows you to track, compare and compete. If someone doesn't like running with music they can just turn the volume down and enjoy the rest of the benefits.'*

Mark's drive to always progress gave us confidence. And I'll never forget when, six months after the launch, one of the most confirmed sceptics from the early days came up to me

'Do we have a product?'

Steve Jobs

and said, 'You know, if I forget to bring my receiver I don't go for a run. It feels like it's wasted, because I don't get the miles added on nikeplus.com.'

That says a lot about the value of innovation and the guts to move forward, even though the intended outcome can never be guaranteed.

Another proud moment for us was when Steve Jobs said, a few months after the launch:

> *'On this project I always viewed Apple as the engineers and Nike as the marketeers, but I have to say nikeplus.com is pretty amazing, and way smarter than just a piece of marketing.'*

Charlie Denson, President of the Nike Brand, has a saying: 'At Nike we have the patience of a two-year-old and the memory of an eighty-year-old.' He always encourages us to get going. Fast.

Our Digital Sport team is launching a number of innovative experiences at a faster pace than ever just because we have a management team that embraces (and pushes) rapid proto-typing. We created the Nike+ SportWatch GPS in only eleven months. It changed the perception of running watches and disrupted the marketplace when we decided that a running watch should look cool, as well as having superior functionality. And the USB connector should be built into the wristband itself because no one needs another cable to connect to the computer. To further accelerate the development, we partnered with TomTom, the GPS experts, rather than trying to figure it all out ourselves.

Ajaz: Nature has a lot of the answers for enterprise. The universe, for example, is constantly expanding outwards. When you have new people, with a diverse range of backgrounds and experiences, entering an organisation, you have a flowing river rather than a stagnant reservoir. Biological organisms rely on an ecosystem. By designing adaptable social structures within a community of interacting individuals and their environment, organisations will create meaningful collaboration that is essential for any company to thrive.

Stefan: That's absolutely vital. Smart partnerships and sometimes acquisitions are crucial if you intend to operate with Velocity. Thinking that you can figure it all out yourself is, as they would say in *Star Trek*, futile.

You can only do that right if you know your consumer. Which is why another big part of the 'easier done than said' approach is that you must be a 'super-user' of your product. To a very large degree, you are your customer, or ought to be. Then, because you've been living and breathing this stuff as a super-user, you do what you think is right as a creator, as a product developer.

Finally, you invite the outside world in and refine your intuition with other people's insights.

At a bare minimum, you always have to think of yourself as the user of your product, and passionately love it.

And whenever I say 'user', by the way, I'm not simply talking about the end customer, the purchaser. I'm talking about us, at Nike, as the producer. We are also customers. We must be the super-users of what we make and produce, whether it's a new basketball shoe, running jacket or a smartphone app.

When we formed the Digital Sport team we'd gather every Wednesday morning on Nike's campus to work out together. We'd also buy whatever new running, fitness or sport app or device had launched during the week. We tested the new stuff – ours and our competition's – and then talked it over together at breakfast. It gave us a chance to test our own stuff, as well as develop a first-hand feeling for the strengths and weaknesses of our competition's products.

This is so much more valuable than commissioning some consultant to tell you the same thing. You have to live it, to truly distil real insights. It's easy to dismiss competition, especially being the market leader – even though we know that's usually a recipe for disaster in the world of sports.

But I truly believe that there is always something to learn, even from the crappiest of executions. If nothing else, they tell you what to avoid.

Ajaz: Successful companies retain the 'market stall mentality' they had when they were small to remain as close as possible to the customer. Contrast this with a corporate approach that might have lost touch. Instead of being focused on the basics, they prefer the comforts of buzzwords.

One of the most loved retailers is J.Crew. Mickey Drexler is CEO and has been called 'the merchant prince of retail'. He even has a loudspeaker system installed at the company's New York HQ because in his industry he can't waste time waiting around for people to call him back. In addition to sharing his thoughts at the exact moment he has them, he is able to pipe in customers to speak to everyone too. It's no surprise that Mickey is also on Apple's board of directors.

Stefan: I don't think it's a coincidence that Apple and Drexler get along so well. They share an amazingly fine-tuned ability to predict what matters to people, as well as a trust in their refined instincts and taste.

Informed intuition is worth a thousand times more than any commissioned research papers. It's like when Michael Jordan

'We have the patience of a two-year-old and the memory of an eighty-year-old.'

Charlie Denson, Nike

strips the ball from Karl Malone in game six in the 1998 NBA Finals against Utah Jazz, with the clock ticking down. He doesn't have to think. He feels in his entire body exactly where to move, and senses exactly how long to keep the ball before taking the game-winning shot.

Ajaz: People are taught to spend a lot of time deliberating decisions or gathering information. To put logic and reason ahead of 'feeling'. But there's a balance to be achieved. Through their people, organisations must learn to develop and trust intuition. It is exactly this ability to understand something, or consider it likely, without the need for conscious reasoning that has evolved to guide and protect us.

Stefan: The writer Malcolm Gladwell describes a process of rapid cognition instead of intuition where our minds take about two seconds to jump to a series of conclusions. He argues that because this is thinking, but only faster, it is rational behaviour. If we don't benefit from rapid cognition, from our inner voice – when we don't act when we feel we should or when we go ahead when we feel we should hesitate – it can lead to decisions that are horribly misplaced.

Ajaz: Credible consultants and business schools avoid the freshest fad or 'management by voodoo'. But by being too focused on the measurable, it can be easy to neglect that niggling feeling even though, as Gladwell argues, they can help us make the right judgements.

Stefan: This sounds like a lead-in to the Segway story.

Ajaz: As far as I'm concerned, the Segway – the two-wheeled gyroscopic pedestrian transport machine – is the archetypal example of a failure to observe the 'easier done than said' precept. It had high-profile financial backing and, caught between the emerging beta world and the hype-driven, top-down promotional logic of the twentieth century, it became a laughing stock.

Before anybody had even seen it, more had been said about the Segway than any one design could ever actually live up to. The Segway was kind of anointed as being the future of transport. The company was extremely successful at raising money and, with plenty of cash to spend, they thought it would be wiser to develop the Segway behind closed doors. They took a long time to do that, and then they launched it grandly.

Stefan: There are tons of theories as to why Segway failed. The lesson remains the same, though: had they iterated, they might not have failed. At the very least, they'd have failed less spectacularly and more cheaply.

I found an article from a meeting between Steve Jobs, Amazon's Jeff Bezos and the Segway developers.

It's published in the *Harvard Business Review*, which, let's agree, is very reputable. Steve Jobs explained:

> *'Its shape is not innovative, it's not elegant, it doesn't feel anthropomorphic ... There are design firms out there that could come up with things we've never thought of.'*

Bezos basically concurred ... Jobs explained that the machine's outer form wasn't innovative or elegant even though its engineering was. He said he could get design shops to have a look at it and come up with things that would 'make you shit your pants'. Bezos basically concurred, saying they'd 'do a disservice to the machine' if a great design firm wasn't given the opportunity to give it a form that would get you excited.

The thing is, Bezos suggested a slow, iterative launch, but Jobs pointed out the net had made an off-radar slow start hard. People would find out snippets, and speculate on more. He suggested considering a trial at ten college campuses and 'maybe' at Disney too. But the net also meant that one person who'd hurt himself, or one angry online reviewer, could then damn the Segway before its release, with the public still unable to see differently for themselves – so even such a small-scale trial was too risky.

Ajaz: I think the first media description I heard of it was as 'the future of transport'. What can live up to that billing when it finally arrives? It got caught at that moment between old-fashioned hype and the new reality of digital exposure, and those instinctive concerns about its look.

Stefan: Those weren't the only instinctive reactions that might have tempered the hype. *Time* magazine published a big article when the Segway was finally unveiled. Near the end of it there was a telling story about Segway's inventor Dean Kamen trying to get Bezos to buy some machines for the Amazon warehouse. 'Walking is a superb mechanism for getting around,' Bezos told the magazine. 'I don't see it being replaced anytime soon.'

Ajaz: That's why it's still a valuable story, isn't it? Segway appeared as the very idea of a traditional launch strategy was beginning to unravel, because you could no longer hide a big project from the world without risking chatter about it leaking on to the net.

Stefan: The fact remains, it would have taken only the smallest amount of sincere feedback to tell the Segway people the biggest flaw in their plan, the one Bezos and Jobs had already pointed out ...

Velocity is
about seizing the
momentum of
a beta world in
perpetual motion.

Ajaz: ... that anyone using one didn't exactly look cool? Even though first-mover advantage can get the headlines, second-mover advantage can get the market share. There are advantages to be gained from letting somebody else go first, learning from the shortcomings of the prototype that's effectively in a live beta. Unless a first-mover can capture the imagination with an idea, protect it and supply their innovation at scale, a competitor is able to take the same idea and benefit from their distribution channels.

Stefan: Innovation is absolutely not the same as originality, which, as you said, has its drawbacks. Velocity is about seizing the momentum of a beta world in perpetual motion.

Ajaz: John Harvey-Jones was a respected icon of business success in England when I was a kid. In his book *Reflections on Leadership* he says making it happen is the biggest challenge in management, where the objective should not be maintaining the status quo, but changing your company as quickly as is feasible:

> *'One has to accept that in life there's always at least evens chance that one is going the wrong way ... but all of us are aware that a lot of businesses aren't going anywhere at all. This is indeed the most dangerous situation of all.'*

It's easier done than said

Get going. Then get better.

Figure out what your customers want before they do

Be an observer as well as an inventor. Take account of the world not just as it is, but how you want it to be. Be interested in what's going on so your antennae are fine-tuned to the distant signals coming your way.

Be beta now and get better tomorrow

Do and Learn, don't Wait and See. Get started and be prepared to improve as you go. Being 'beta' doesn't mean dropping your responsibilities on to users, or that it's ever okay to put out something sub-par. It means first making sure you truly 'have a product', and *then* making it better. Pick a clear target. Reassess. Now go again.

Unite and rule

Smart collaborations and pooled expertise are a hallmark of Velocity success stories. If you spend years researching a new area rather than going direct to an expert in the field with a proposal for collaborating right away, chances are somebody else will steal your thunder before your project gets off the ground.

Make the leap from saying to doing

Mantras are cheap. Meaning what you say is priceless. Don't tell me you're funny, tell me a joke. Your mission should stem from your convictions, not your copywriting department. Nobody cares what you say you do until you show that you do it. Do what you promised you would and everybody loves you.

THE BEST ADVERTISING ISN'T ADVERTISING

Wondering which half of your ad spend is wasted? Velocity says: 'Wrong question. Try again.' Instead of just interrupting people, serve them and make them feel something. Sorry, but that takes longer than thirty seconds.

Make meaningful connections.

Ajaz: You have part of my attention. You have the minimum amount.

Stefan: Sorry?

Ajaz: That line from *The Social Network* articulates in one sentence the voice of a generation, especially when it comes to advertising.

Stefan: Or when Sean Parker says to Mark Zuckerberg: 'You don't want to ruin it with ads because ads aren't cool.' And Mark replies: 'Exactly.'

Ajaz: When we started the company, some agencies saw the web as brochureware. We saw it as software. But even as far back as 2005, before mobile apps became interesting and accessible enough to make people want to multitask the way everyone does now, the *Guardian* newspaper did an experiment. It showed the average person in London is exposed to over 3,500 marketing messages in a day and 99 per cent of these ads have no impact. Too many messages, too many channels, too much clutter.

Stefan: People just filter out the junk in preference for something that will interest them. And yet, traditional advertising is a massive portion of most marketing budgets, cramming messaging in front of consumers when they are largely not paying attention.

The definition for advertising on Wikipedia reads:

> *'Advertising is a form of communication used to persuade an audience (viewers, readers or listeners) to take some action.'*

Now, if we agree with that definition, we have a disconnect between what Velocity can enable, and the role of advertising as we know it.

I'm no historian, but I'm pretty sure the original purpose of it was all about convenience for the receiver of the message. Whether carved in rock or painted on walls, it was a way to communicate simply where someone could find a product or service. It aligned supply and demand. Similarly, branding was a way of verifying that a certain person or company either owned or made a particular trusted commodity.

Today we have an opportunity to tailor the message and create services that benefit the receiver. As we know what you and your friends care about, and what you're looking for, we can be much smarter about filtering out stuff people don't care about.

Ajaz: We're in the age of connectedness. The solution is to create work that people want to share. Ideas that define culture rather than follow it. At the same time organisations need to harness data so there's relevance. I think NikeiD – which enables people to design and personalise products – is a great example.

Stefan: We launched the service on the web in 1999. Now it's available on mobile and in-store where professional designers in NikeiD Studios help people configure their ideal product. It's been an incredibly influential service that many brands have been inspired by.

Ajaz: It's an example of brand building through serving, rather than interrupting through an ad.

Stefan: We have never felt like we are making ads. We are about inspiring and enabling people with the power of sports. And this is a massive point of differentiation. We're not chasing eyeballs. The goal is to create connections with our customers and earn their loyalty by serving them. The better the service, the stronger the connection.

'Advertising is the price you pay for having an unremarkable product or service.'

Jeff Bezos, Amazon.com

Ajaz: Jeff Bezos is quoted as saying:

'Advertising is the price you pay for having an unremarkable product or service.'

I think it's because entrepreneurs are looking for what investments will reap the greatest returns. They know that there is infinite opportunity, but finite resource. So for Amazon, instead of creating jingles and straplines, they put their money into better choice, service and fulfilment. This clearly has a more lasting impact on the business than an ad campaign.

Stefan: The entire model has flipped. For Nike, it means celebrating sport and activity across everything we do. We help people 'Just Do It' by focusing on products and services that deliver athletic insight, sometimes as inspiration, sometimes as motivation.

Ajaz: One of our clients is the CEO of a games company. At our last catch-up he told me that his company used to rely on the saliency of a media brand to help create equity for their products. The difference now, he says, is that consumers and the numbers tell him that his brands have more saliency.

Stefan: It's the same at Nike. If we were to add up the digital connections we have with our consumers – so all the

Facebook pages for our brands and our athletes; all the Twitter and Instagram feeds; all the websites; all the mobile apps – we have hundreds of millions of connections available directly, unfiltered to our audiences. When you add retail to that we have considerably more. These are permissions that we respect. Because there's close to zero cost for the distribution, it's our responsibility to invest more in an idea or service we're delivering to benefit our consumer.

Ajaz: The old advertising ecosystem where marketers subsidise media in exchange for the chance to make an impression on consumers has fragmented and is disintegrating.

Stefan: Media owners sold a mass audience to advertisers. They were able to aggregate millions of people into one place and show them commercial messages by creating content that people found compelling. That model has broken down because there's an abundance of media choice.

Ajaz: And because people can download and access whatever they want, whenever they want. So no one is ruled by a broadcaster's schedule.

Stefan: Live TV for sports or reality show results still draw the crowds. There are people saying that 'television is finished' or 'radio is finished', but that's not the case. It's evolving and being added to. The current model is being challenged and under pressure but TV isn't de̶ commercial medium. It's a great way to deliver em̶ inspiring stories. But for a generation of audiences their i̶ of TV or radio isn't a screen on the wall or a box in the corner, it's an app on their phone or tablet. They still want access to familiar channels and new content.

Ajaz: One media does not necessarily displace another one either. They tend to co-exist. TV did not displace radio. Another example is that among the many benefits of computers was the promise of the paperless office. For most organisations it has yet to be delivered, even though they all have computers. So as the old media moves over, it does not necessarily mean it will move out, although it does get repositioned.

Stefan: Models for advertising have been about paying a media owner for access to mass-market eyeballs. Digital media is adept at addressing specific, individually tailored needs. It shouldn't have to interrupt your day, instead it should be of service to you.

Ajaz: Innovative media owners with scale and reach have the opportunity to price at a premium because they offer customers items of specific interest or relevance.

Stefan: It's happening now.

Ajaz: Everyone is familiar with search engines, like Google, where you buy certain words that might target a potential customer. People won't see the ads unless they type the keyword into the search engine. The position of the ad depends on how much you bid for a particular keyword compared to the competition. A higher bid buys a more visible position. These ads work because they are context relevant; when you search, you are ready to take action.

With social networks, you target ads based on specific criteria like audience demographics, age, education, gender and interests. It's also the brand pages for fans that companies like Nike, Converse, Disney, Burberry and Red Bull have set up that provide visibility. If a user chooses to 'Like' a brand's fan page, the consumer is raising their hand and giving the organisation permission to keep in touch. It might take the form of 'sponsored stories' or announcements that appear within a person's news feed, among other new updates from friends, rather than in a pure advertising context.

It's become an instantaneous tool for brands to reach people who have shown affinity. It's also about the multiplier effect of connections where because one of your friends recommends a particular brand, it's also influential to you.

Organisations predominantly benefit from two unique aspects of social media. The first is that the customer has self-elected to be an advocate for a particular brand so they

The goal is to create connections with our customers and earn their loyalty by serving them.

will be more likely to engage in conversations and share stories with friends in their social group. The second is that a brand can target audiences based on an individual's personal preferences.

Stefan: Social media can be a fantastic listening tool for companies to react and solve a consumer problem. This gets the audience engaged right away, creating delight. Again, it's about serving, so a brand can make adjustments, tweaks and improvements. It's about capturing inputs and then creating a new approach that's built around connections of value to the consumers.

Ajaz: This approach understands the key moments and most important touch points that will have the biggest influence on helping the customer. It means including customer-created and shared conversations as well as those initiated by the brand.

Stefan: As advertising evolves, it will provide real answers to real questions, not canned information. It will offer interactions and services that satisfy real needs, not blanket persuasions. It will create communities that speak to one another and are not just content with aspirations. And at that point I don't know if 'advertising' is the best way to describe it.

Ajaz: Great brands are about smart and artful storytelling. Great agencies help clients to amplify a brand's authentic voice. Today, the canvas used to connect with audiences has more variations and marketers have more tools available. Communication should have more respect for what the audience gets out of it – how it will inspire, satisfy, motivate and reward them. Rather than bombarding people with messages they scan past or ignore because it's not relevant.

Shaping an attitude and moving people towards action has always had more to do with emotion than function. In the case of deodorant, the product may have the functional benefit of providing 50 per cent more staying power, but it's the implicit, emotional benefit of not having odour or damp patches on a shirt that makes us feel more confident and better about ourselves.

Stefan: It's fascinating to observe how my twelve-year-old son Alex watches TV. He loves sport and follows at least three games at the same time. (With his laptop open and phone in hand, obviously.) But what's interesting is how he immediately switches to another game when the ad break kicks in. He then instinctively knows when to switch back when the game resumes.

We were watching the Portland Trail Blazers basketball team, in a really tight match, and at the break he quickly switched to see another NBA game. When I told him to switch back, because I was sure our game had restarted, he calmly said, 'Dad, it's another four seconds.' When I asked how he knew, he said, 'I just feel it.' The way he manages the remote to avoid ad breaks makes it feel like an Olympic discipline. On the other hand, he'll pull up stuff that has meaning to him and watch it on YouTube and pass it on to his friends with endorsement.

Ajaz: The metrics need to be evaluated from the brand's perspective rather than the media owner's to see what's influencing decisions and having an impact on sales. Regardless of today's numbers, it's also important to have a vision of where the brand could be.

The way brands share their passions and tell stories is only going to get more interesting and exciting as emerging platforms and technologies make new ideas possible. AKQA's co-founder and Chief Creative Officer, James Hilton, who I have worked with for seventeen years, shares his perspective in this conversation.

James: There are loads of widgets in our lives these days, but only so much wonder. Advertising might once have meant ladies in baths eating chocolate bars, or builders drinking cola with their shirts off. Now it means making people lust after your products, not your promotions, by making them elegant, effortless and timeless. It's one thing to do work people can admire. It's another thing to create something they can't wait to be a part of, now.

The best brand advice given to me was when Ajaz and I were working on Nike Run London. As I recall, the meeting went well – but at the end, the Nike team told us they thought we could do even better, saying:

'Always go too far. If you go too far we can bring it back if we need to. Don't go far enough and we'll always be disappointed.'

It taught me how the world's most innovative brands get to where they are – they aren't afraid. Or more specifically, they are afraid – of being like everyone else. To achieve what others can't, they must do what others won't.

Nike does not create advertising. Nike creates wonder. Wonder is a powerful emotion, because however long the moment lasts for – an hour, a minute, or just a couple of seconds – it stays with you.

Ajaz: Daniel Kahneman, the Nobel laureate and author of *Thinking, Fast and Slow*, says that we get to keep a story from our experiences. In his TED lecture he mentions how a delegate complained that his whole experience of listening to a symphony of glorious music was ruined because right at

As advertising evolves it will offer interactions that satisfy real needs, not blanket persuasions.
At that point 'advertising' isn't the best way to describe it.

the very end there was a screeching sound. But Kahneman argues it hadn't wrecked the entire experience. It only spoiled the memory of the experience. The best brands ensure that the memory of every experience is a good one.

James: Doing that isn't easy. But for the brave souls who dare, the creation of wonderful memories which inspire loyalty is their reward. In a world of 'one-hit wonders' we want to create the blockbusters.

Ajaz: Is there a project that captures this spirit?

James: Nike Training Club – a mobile app that's democratised the idea of personal training. So you now can train anywhere with professional fitness coaching – at home, outside, hotels, gyms, work, college. It's been downloaded millions of times all over the world and has accumulated over fifty million minutes of training.

Ajaz: That's fifty million minutes of connection and empowerment for the same price as a thirty-second commercial.

James: The *Wall Street Journal* named the *app* one of their five best *ads* of the year. Nike Training Club isn't advertising, it's a genuine connection that's of service to the user. The majority of reviews on the app store are the maximum five-stars, so it's the audience amplifying the voice of the brand by sharing the ideas Nike contributes. That's Wonder.

Stefan: Ideas that inspire people to pay attention, stimulating their curiosity, rewarding their intelligence and therefore creating an emotional connection, have the greatest engagement.

Ajaz: In addition to engagement we have four additional metrics that help us to measure return on investment to understand if we're moving the needle for clients: increase in brand equity; increase in sales growth; increase in shareholder value; and decrease in overheads through more efficient process improvements.

Stefan: Speaking of metrics, and to get really practical for a second: the concrete on my driveway cracked this summer, and I had no clue where to go, so with Google's help I found ServiceMagic. They match your requirements with screened and approved professionals in all areas of construction. You input your needs – in my case driveway, concrete, smooth finish – and I got three suggestions. I then read the feedback from twenty-five previous consumers. Twenty-three were super-happy, one had a so-so response and one was really disappointed. I dug into the one who was unhappy. The commenter explained that the reason for the low mark was that they didn't think the supplier's English was good enough. I decided to go with that supplier. My English isn't that good either.

Ajaz: How was it?

Stefan: He started working on Saturday morning and had a brand new driveway finished by Monday. So I go in, rate him five stars and as long as he keeps up the good work this will spread and his business will grow.

Ajaz: In an age where transparency is the norm, what matters perhaps more than your wealth is your reputation. In an era of collaborative consumption, where we are increasingly sharing, it's more important to be trustworthy than to be rich.

There are great examples of companies either creating new industries or disrupting established ones. Airbnb, for example, is turning people's homes, apartments, islands, even entire villages and castles, into accommodation for the night or for holiday rentals. It's opened up the supply of rentable accommodation to create a market for owners to make money. It's disruptive because most of the time it's cheaper to stay at an Airbnb property than in a hotel room.

ZipCar, the world's biggest car-sharing service, does the same thing for driving, so if you are not using your car you can rent it out. With public transport fares increasing and rising petrol costs, people are also turning to car-pooling services like BlaBlaCar.com to travel to and from work together. Users get the benefits of lower costs, less impact on the environment, time saved and the happy social aspects of a shared journey rather than the misery of daily anonymous commutes.

TaskRabbit, a bit like ServiceMagic you mentioned, lets you post an errand or chore that you may not want to do. Like wrapping up Christmas presents or putting together furniture from IKEA. Then the TaskRabbits make offers to do it for you and the lowest bid wins.

Using technology to unlock an otherwise unavailable supply of monetisable things is being replicated across categories.

Stefan: Foursquare, the location-based social network for your phone, has evolved into a powerful service. Dennis Crowley and his team have been on a clear path from the beginning – their success was never propelled by interruptive advertising. They grow because their product is valuable. This is from Foursquare.com: 'Make the real world easier to use, Keep up with friends, Discover what's nearby, Save money and unlock rewards.'

We need to rethink the role of advertising. It's about service rather than a persuasive technique. When the web was young, brochures were scanned and uploaded. Then came banner ads, interstitials, superstitials, and so on, taking over your screen. When mobile was new, media companies tried squeezing ads in front of people's tasks. These starting points are wrong.

The premise is that we have a new communication platform, when in reality what we have is *a new connection platform based around what matters in people's lives.* It's an opportunity to make yourself indispensable. And that's not an ad brief.

Ajaz: The perceived shift to 'digital advertising' often gives a false sense of being on it, when in essence the chase of eyeballs has just moved to the web.

I heard an intriguing story of an expensive magazine that was doing well with readers and advertisers at a moment when many publishers were losing money on their digital titles. It turns out that the site had a 'fireplace' ad that was really easy to click on to by mistake, so targets were quickly reached.

Stefan: Never mind that readers never even made a choice.

Ajaz: Right. Lots of them had effectively been tricked. This super-slick magazine, with sophisticated readers, chucked a banana skin at them to make the ad model work.

Stefan: Because it's all about racking up those eyeballs. Which is why using clicks and eyeballs as the measure is so wrong. As one investor said after the flotation of LinkedIn:

> *'We just don't know enough about this industry to know which metric, whether it's clicks or eyeballs or something new, is the correct one.'*

We're in a different state of mind when searching for something on the web than when engaging with friends, playing games, listening to music or using apps. Clearly there is significant commercial opportunity, but it's not about ads coming between you and the things you care about.

Ajaz: If I start to feel assailed by unwanted ads, I'm not going to start loving unwanted ads more. I'm just going to feel less at home. When our landlines became nothing more than an expensive way to be sold a new kitchen or insurance that we don't want by an automated call centre in a faraway land, we found a new friend in our mobiles.

In an age where transparency is the norm, what matters perhaps more than your wealth is your reputation.

When inboxes get overburdened with unwanted interruptions, people go to ad-free worlds to feel more Zen. If the imposition outweighs the convenience, we'll find something else.

Stefan: Even though Nike is one of the most awarded brands, we never thought about it as advertising. It's about creating stories that make deep connections with people who share our passion for sport.

That led to new challenges – like the issue of how to condense an authentic, compelling story into a thirty- or sixty-second slot. We don't have to do that any more; we don't have to stay within the confines of a certain format. With YouTube, we took the time to tell our story the way it should be told.

We created the 'Cross Bar' film in 2005. It came about because we were launching a new boot for Ronaldinho that season, and didn't have a massive media budget, so we decided to try YouTube for the launch.

It was before they were bought by Google and, arguably, before the advent of 'viral' as we now know it. The video was two minutes and forty-five seconds long. Chad Hurley, co-founder of YouTube, mentioned it being the first video to hit a million views. I don't think we would call it advertising. It just got passed around because people loved it. And they liked to argue whether or not it was real.

For this generation, YouTube is way more important than TV. The comments you get on YouTube are great, candid and give you a pretty good sense of whether or not you're striking a chord. I love the unfiltered feedback.

It's sometimes painful, but you can't be afraid of it, and it's something we learn a lot from. In 2010 we launched our World Cup campaign exclusively on Facebook and YouTube. It centred around a superb three-minute film, and we had millions of views even before it went on TV.

I think one reason we progress is because we never get caught up in the latest fad. We just try to think of the best way to serve our consumer, and find partners who can help us find the right way to make a meaningful connection.

I was reading some consumer research on which brands teens consider cool and, not surprisingly, Facebook was in the top three. I've never seen an ad for Facebook. Ten years ago, it would have been impossible to occupy this position in young people's minds without a great chunk of advertising. Today, cool comes with being useful, interesting, well designed and offering something indispensable.

Ajaz: Brands that have authentic, believable values use the spirit and energy of those convictions to ease effortlessly into any new environment. Even with a pre-digital heritage, they've found interesting methods and ideas to express their stories.

There's the luxury brand Ralph Lauren. The proposition is all about dreams of what you aspire to be. Ralph Lauren has created these beautifully art-directed dream-like worlds that personify the magnetic glamour of the movies. The world created by Ralph is one that's alluring, attractive but entirely unattainable except by very few people. That desire for prestige is exactly the draw. People want what they can't have. Ralph is so confident of what they're about that they've been able to translate those dreams, those stories, into digital. Ralph Lauren projected a movie on to their London store – basically a $1.5-million film that made the façade of their Bond Street flagship store 'disappear'. There were almost three-quarters of a billion media impressions of that one event. As one analyst told *Fortune*:

'You could do a roadshow and never reach that many people.'

You get the emotion because people respond to conviction.

Stefan: In an interview with *Time* a few years ago, Nike's VP of Brand and Categories, Trevor Edwards, said, 'We're not in the business of keeping media companies happy.'

Which is another way of saying 'we're in the business of serving consumers and will never do things a certain way just because they've always been done that way'. Velocity replaces most old models because the emotional payoff and true value delivered from services beats ads.

I love seeing the smile on people's faces the first time they try the 'cheer me on' feature on the Nike+ GPS mobile app. It's so simple and yet so powerful. You share with your Facebook friends that you're going for a run and want them to cheer you on. Now every time someone likes or comments on your run you hear a stadium roar over your music in real time. It's incredibly powerful when a friend three thousand miles away can 'be there' with you to push you through your run. I can never resist looking at my phone during a run to see who is cheering me on.

People do people stuff. They gab. They gossip. Word of mouth is still the best form of marketing – just as it was three hundred years ago.

Ajaz: That's a challenge and an opportunity for today's social platforms: creating a mechanism that enables the digital word of mouth from people's social endorsements to reach millions of individuals at the same time.

Stefan: You've got to be interested in people. That way, you can actually learn what it takes to be interesting *to* them. It comes back to another natural behaviour that humans have been doing for millennia, which is storytelling. People have done that for as long as they've been able to speak because, again, it's a way to survive. Don't go near the woolly mammoth. Don't eat the yellow snow. All kinds of myths and stories that pass on knowledge about the world and its mysteries.

So when you're producing an app, for instance, it's got to take someone on a journey, it's got to follow a narrative arc. In language theory there's an argument that language began with our ancestors grunting to themselves when they couldn't figure something out. Eventually, others listened and made sense of their tales of frustration. Then, they were able to communicate and pass on knowledge. First I had this challenge, then I did this, and this is how I got to the happy ending.

If you think that stories began as a tool, like fire or flint, then in a sense it's come full circle: our job now is becoming one of telling you a great story and leaving you with something that helps you navigate the world, too. And an experience is a story. It's moved beyond a film to an eco-system of products, services and content that work in harmony to make you feel, and do.

Ajaz: The best agencies are the best storytellers. With low-interest categories such as junk foods or soft drinks it's often about creating some other kind of appeal because, let's face it, there isn't much you can say about them. But people don't just buy products for the purpose they serve, but for the values they embody. So organisations with bland products, like soap, have to create an aura or personality for them to stand out. Often it means creating a kind of mythology or legend about the product or the company that probably owes more to entertainment, aspiration or intrigue than it does truth. As *The Economist* puts it:

> *'Human behaviour remains mysterious, and there is still no certain way to persuade people to buy a particular brand of soap.'*

In the case of higher-interest categories, it's the agency's job to uncover truths about a product or company and articulate those in an interesting way. Here's where I want to talk about a project we did for Fiat.

Fiat is Europe's most eco-friendly car company and part of the reason for this is that they make smaller cars.

We have a belief that, unless it inspires, contributes or informs, marketing is pollution. And there is a certain irony about doing adverts to celebrate the fact a company is ecologically friendly. It doesn't make any sense at all. So press, outdoor or TV ads just wouldn't be right as that would have been contributing to carbon emissions, rather than making any kind of effort to reduce them.

Over 70,000 drivers in eco:Ville have saved over five million kilos of CO_2. That's gotta be better than any high score.

So we thought, what better way to celebrate the fact that Fiat is the most eco-friendly car company than by inventing something that would make drivers even more considerate? So we devised an idea called eco:Drive which collects your real-world driving facts and figures as you travel. When you then review that data on your computer or phone, a proprietary algorithm analyses your gear changes, acceleration and braking habits, calculating your 'eco:Index' – a scoring of your carbon footprint. It also offers advice on your driving style, quantifies how much good you'll do for the environment and tells you how much money you'll save if you follow the programme's suggestions for saving fuel.

Stefan: I bet that got people's attention.

Ajaz: Definitely, because you are looking at an average annual saving of £480 per driver. Meanwhile, online at eco:Ville, we introduced a collaborative element where you can compare your eco:Index with that of others, around the world, and see what you're collectively saving.

An industry White Paper calculated that thirty-seven billion litres of fuel would be saved in the EU each year if all its drivers were eco:Drivers, a saving of £43 billion. That's around the same amount the EU spends on renewable energy.

Stefan: Was there any bad feedback with that? Like, did people try to blame you for being late for work or not braking in time?

Ajaz: It turns out they were actually paying more attention, driving more smartly and more alertly when they used eco:Drive so they shortened their journey times, saving more fuel.

Stefan: The big statistical thing that always comes up about attitudes to the environment is how the size of the problem makes us feel our efforts are insignificant.

When they're polled about recycling, people think their neighbours aren't doing it, or they just feel helpless about changing anything. You stand there rinsing out a half-dozen cartons and cans, wondering how one person's token effort can help save the world. But you give people a clear, actionable report on how to save gas, and then put that into the context of many thousands of others – so suddenly they can at last see the impact of their efforts and that they *are* making a change. They're a character in the story, but they're also part of a bigger narrative. That's the kind of thing Velocity makes possible.

Ajaz: Right. You couldn't have done it before. There were over 70,000 drivers in eco:Ville when I last checked, and they'd saved five million kilos of CO_2. That's gotta be better than any high score.

Innovations like eco:Drive are also influencing a new era of mobility where cars become much more than getting from one place to another. The car is evolving to become self-aware of what's happening to it, its environment and the driver.

Stefan: You haven't done any of these projects with software engineering alone. There's a passion, and that's what really matters – evoking emotion. We're talking about human behaviour, and people respond to theatre.

Ajaz: Football is the theatre of dreams. Working with Heineken, we wanted to find an interesting way to share the brand's passion as a sponsor of the UEFA Champions League. While we were thinking about the challenge, we discovered an interesting truth, a fact that would inspire the idea. We learned that around 70 per cent of Champions League matches are watched by people at home while multi-tasking, just like your son Alex.

So we launched a world first, a football game that's live and you play using your mobile phone or social network while the match is on. Called Heineken StarPlayer, it allows players to predict what will happen at key moments in the

match to score points. It combines the excitement of antici-
pation, the power of participation and the novelty of 'live'.

StarPlayer works in real time, with players invited to forecast the outcome of corners, free kicks and penalties,
choosing between a number of options. Different point
scores are awarded depending on the likelihood of the
outcome. Players also have the chance to guess when goals
will be scored – at the start of the game they are given eight
chances to predict whether there will be a goal in the next
thirty seconds, with points awarded on a sliding scale depending on how early the goal is anticipated.

To add to the sense of competition, players can form leagues
with their mates, and share their scores via Facebook. They
are also awarded badges for successfully predicting the
events of a game.

It's a project that can get ninety minutes or more of engagement rather than thirty seconds from a TV commercial.

Stefan: The digital distribution mechanism is as much a
part of the message as the idea.

Ajaz: VW has always embraced the most relevant media of
a particular age to share its stories. In the print age VW
created beautifully written, irreverent ads that defined the

genre. VW's commercials are charming films people talk about and share. But this is about when we worked with VW to launch the new GTI.

Our take was that the GTI has a particular appeal to the tech-aware younger male driver, who's more obsessed with his iPhone than any TV show. So let's skip the traditional media and head straight for his pocket. Launching a new car, let alone one of this stature, exclusively on iPhone had never been done before. Volkswagen went with it. We teamed up with game developer Firemint, and created Real Racing GTI, an iPhone game.

At launch it was a phenomenon. Downloaded over ten million times, number one app in thirty-six countries and an instant top trending topic on Twitter. VW sold every GTI initially manufactured, significantly increased its future customer order book and delighted millions of people by contributing enjoyment in the form of an entertaining game that articulated the car's character to a community of fans.

Stefan: Gaming in general has a lot to teach us about how to make meaningful connections. There was that big fuss in 2008 when, for the first time, games revenues outstripped cinema takings in the States. That same switch happened in the UK the year after, incidentally.

But for all that, I've still seen little indication of people from other sectors really looking closely at the field and seeing what it's got that they haven't. Which is weird: games have been amazing digital, interactive experiences for so long.

Ajaz: We can learn a lot from video-game designers. Consider what the game designer's job is, in the case of a modern classic like *Grand Theft Auto* or *Call of Duty*. They have to make a visually stimulating, engaging world to draw the player in. They've got to balance eye candy and atmosphere with clear navigability and information for the player. It's about finding a sweet spot between the finesse of what is known as an 'on-rails' experience (easy to progress through, with a clear linear path) and a 'free-roaming' one where the user can decide where to go next.

Game designers have to make control intuitive and easy, provide rewards and convey a structured sense of achieving something. But at the same time, they also need to give the users room to improvise and express themselves.

Influential artists like Picasso or Warhol were able to craft technology and technique into stories. Given the craftsmanship that goes into today's top titles, the interactive storytelling and atmospheric immersion they enable, digital games are arguably a new art form.

They combine the audio-visual capabilities of film, human insights of great literature, unlimited creative possibilities of animation and interactivity that is unique to the genre.

Stefan: Now, as games increasingly move off discs and into always-online models, and thrive in environments like Facebook, there is often no 'product' as such: nothing to buy in a case, nothing to pay for. Most games today have to be logged into to be played at all. And the interaction has moved beyond the game and the player, to the game and its millions of players. So the game is nothing more than a *service* that, through clever design, connects people through a shared interest.

The games industry is transitioning to a model that is also relevant to all of us, because all thriving brands will, by definition, have to become 'service' brands, in some sense. Through that service, they have to make their customers' lives better, or at least easier.

Ajaz: Although play is among the most natural of human behaviours, we don't mean turn everything into a game. Even when we designed the user experience and menu system for the Xbox, our guiding theme was 'the interface should not be a game' because we wanted it to be intuitive, not challenging.

Brands shouldn't misunderstand a buzzword like 'game-ification' so that it starts producing a set of mini-games, instead of fixing their e-commerce on mobile or improving customer service. The priority should be enhancing the core business, not creating more stuff. But the customer, in some way, wants to feel like the protagonist of your brand story. The hero of your game.

Stefan: As opposed to the victim of your campaign. And that, in short, is the argument we've made here, and one we feel very strongly is the correct one.

What better way to close than with Marshall McLuhan, writing in the sixties, about what the 'information revolution' meant for advertising:

> *'When all production and all consumption are brought into pre-established harmony with all desire and effort, then advertising will have liquidated itself by its own success.'*

In the age of connectedness the solution is to create ideas that people want to share.

The best advertising isn't advertising

Make meaningful connections.

Create wonder

Aim to produce the labours of love, the pockets of excitement, the stuff that just rivets people in unexpected ways. The magic is in the product, the values and spirit of the brand, so seek to amplify these truths in an interesting, consistent voice across multiple customer touch points. Wonder is the destination. Velocity is the vehicle.

New media needs new thinking

Don't retrofit traditional mechanics into new formats. Don't chase or get blinded by the latest buzzwords. Instead focus on creating fame and familiarity in the hearts and minds of audiences. Use digital tools to provide the kind of powerful, relevant and accessible customer benefits that analogue cannot reach.

Briefs should be

Briefs are called that for a reason. Long-winded, verbose instruction documents that are pages long are time-consuming, oxygen-consuming and don't help anyone. Focus on your desired outcomes, not your essay-writing skills.

Counting clicks isn't what counts

If click counts are all that dictate your decisions, you're shutting out your chance to make a real connection. The metrics that move the needle and matter most are: consumer connection, brand equity, sales and shareholder value.

Convenient
IS THE
ENEMY
OF
RIGHT

Velocity needs you to be streamlined. The requisite craftsmanship takes perseverance and discipline. Obsess over important details, and edit ferociously.

Never have anything to apologise for.

Ajaz: For some reason a particular local council had taken it upon itself to persecute young people in their bus shelter advertising. The headline of the ad said something like: 'What does dropping litter make you look like?' and the picture showed a teenager's face with a snout for a nose. Putting aside the fact that the ad is in really poor taste, the other problem was that on the road where I saw the posters there was nowhere you could chuck away your rubbish. The council found it more convenient to run a few ads instead of doing the right thing, which is to invest that ad production and media money into installing a few permanent litter bins where there aren't any.

Stefan: They were producing more rubbish and therefore making the problem worse.

Ajaz: A characteristic of human behaviour is that we tend to make the most convenient decision, not necessarily the right one. I think it's even possible to categorise people and organisations into two kinds: either process or product. So the process people or companies go through the motions, a checklist of what they believe needs to be done for a particular task. It's more convenient just to follow a set of instructions. The product people, on the other hand, know that you can't create a great product without discipline and rigour, but they are more obsessed with the end result, rather than just the process. I think it's right to focus on the product, the desired outcome.

Stefan: Sometimes technology makes things a little too convenient. Take email – although I do remember a time before email, I have a great deal of difficulty doing so because it has become such a feature, such a fixture, of my daily life. Later on today, I will 'do email' for a couple of hours. And when I open my inbox, like most of us I'll have 170 messages, of which five will be truly important. Many of the rest will be ones where people have cc'd me. Why did they cc me? Because it was easy. It was free (to them, at least) – there was no stamp to buy and no time investment to make in addressing another envelope.

Ajaz: The other night on Facebook I saw a brilliant status message from a friend who runs a design company. It said: 'I sent a total of 23,432 emails in 2011. Because that's what I do. I send emails.' One of his friends replied in the thread below: 'That's only 64 a day ... you can do better.'

Sending emails has become more 'the thing' than actually 'doing the thing'. There's instant messaging or internal corporate social-networking to foster collaboration and cut down on emails. But fundamentally it's about conversations which lead to decisions. A phone call can still do that in a more useful, memorable and natural way. Who has time to read every email? We might skim them. What is cc supposed to stand for anyway?

Stefan: Haven't a clue. Let's ask Wikipedia … It says carbon copy, or courtesy copy. I'm sticking to the first one. Can't see much courtesy in it these days. Cc'ing used to be a big deal because you'd gone to unusual effort, paid for the extra postage and printing; and, like you say, serious – it used to be the next best thing to a lawyer's letter.

Velocity should encourage us to make some changes in our mentality: just because we can do something doesn't mean we should.

Too often, technology seems to mimic Dawkins' 'selfish gene', whose prime directive is to promote itself.

Ajaz: This tendency for technology to make itself important and to pull people off track has intensified of late, but it's been an issue in business forever. Alan 'Ace' Greenberg was chairman of the investment bank Bear Stearns. He was also famous for sending company-wide memos …

Just because we can do something doesn't mean we should.

Stefan: I have to say, the company-wide memo sounds suspiciously like the analogue ancestor of 'cc all'.

Ajaz: These weren't about a meaningless cc culture. They were about patrolling the border between convenience and counterproductive laziness. Greenberg would exhort his employees to reuse paperclips, share fax machines, return clients' phone calls promptly and otherwise be considerate to people and conservative with resources with a mixture of humour and appeals to the staff's self-respect.

When Greenberg heard how his bankers were driving the company's receptionists crazy by constantly calling the front desk to be connected to colleagues – even though they each had a directory on their desk – he sent this memo:

To: Sr Managing Directors, Managing Directors, Associate Directors

From: Alan C. Greenberg

The in-house telephone operators are being swamped by our own associates dialing the Bear Stearns operator and asking to be connected to another Bear Stearns employee. All of us have been given Bear Stearns directories ... There are two reasons these directories are not being used:

Laziness

Not being able to read.

He also explained that any employees having the second problem could turn to a new kind of expert, one of which he would situate on every floor: an 'H.I.' or 'helper of illiterates', whom employees could call across to them by title if they needed their assistance.

Meanwhile, Greenberg explained, the phone operators would log the names of those who persistently called to ask for colleagues' numbers, adding, 'If those people are literate, they will meet with me'. He just left that thought hanging there for persistent offenders.

Stefan: Brilliant. Sounds a bit like being sent to the naughty corner at school.

Ajaz: Except because it went to everybody, nobody could feel picked on and those who were innocent could just laugh at the gentle mocking. We all need the occasional hint to stop and think about how we interact.

The way I saw it, he didn't want to demoralise, ridicule or chastise his staff. He wanted to remind them why it was in their interest to up their game. It's not about telling people 'You're rubbish', but rather about reminding them 'You're better than that'.

Stefan: I think we all need a dose of that every now and then.

Ajaz: Anyway, today software should make the whole process redundant. But that only happens when someone has put the effort in of making it easier than a previous method.

So that my team knew what was important to me I felt obliged to give my own gentle reminders in the early days. They weren't funny like Greenberg's were, but years later people still remind me of some of the emails I sent. One particular email I wrote over ten years ago had the subject 'The Courage to Care'.

It did go on a bit, I admit, so I'll just read a paragraph from the beginning and the end:

> 'It takes more courage to care about a client and a project than it does not to care. We all have days that don't go too well. But these should never stop us being professional, because that is why we are in business …'

> 'Most of all, the courage to care is about taking responsibility for projects, because you have enough pride in that project to ensure it is the best it can possibly be … not because we have to, but because we want to. Because it is the right thing to do.'

I want to create a culture where we are rigorous and on the ball. You can't do that with threats or fear. You can only achieve it by championing a certain set of values, ensuring consistent behaviours and restoring responsibility to the individual.

Stefan: The craving for convenience that most people have is fairly understandable, though. Like water, humans have a tendency to take the path of least resistance. That's a fact we always bear in mind at Nike when we consider our customers – but never when we look at ourselves. One of the truisms about the Velocity world is that making life easier for others usually means making life difficult for yourself; delivering convenient solutions means working really, really hard. And because that isn't natural human behaviour (except perhaps for you), we have to drill and discipline ourselves week in, week out, to honour that insight.

Ajaz: Because forcing yourself constantly to go beyond the merely 'necessary' is a matter of setting a rhythm, of establishing an everyday habit of going to exceptional lengths. As Brian Wilson, lead singer and songwriter of the Beach Boys said: 'Beware the lollipop of mediocrity; lick it once and you'll suck forever.'

Stefan: That's why it's so important, when you set out to accomplish something great, that you keep a standard in

'Beware the lollipop of mediocrity; lick it once and you'll suck forever.'

Brian Wilson, The Beach Boys

mind, something which inspires you and which you hope, in some way, to rival. All the better if it's tangible and simple enough to capture in a single point of reference.

Ajaz: That's also true in product design. When Charles and Ray Eames, who constantly made use of new materials, released the now iconic Lounge Chair in 1956 after years of development, they were emulating a baseball glove. Charles's vision was for a chair with:

> *'the warm, receptive look of a well-used first baseman's mitt'.*

The Eames Lounge Chair is now part of the permanent collection of the New York Museum of Modern Art.

Stefan: A pure, simple reference; but not simple to achieve. That's why the finished form has become a classic. The strength and simplicity of the original idea stopped the culture of convenience from encroaching on the purity of the ambition, and the finished product was faithful enough to its inspiration that the end user – the person who saw the chair – intuitively felt that connection, too.

Ajaz: It is the refusal to compromise on execution that makes the final product great. And that is anything but straightforward. However singular and straightforward your references or inspirations, innovation is inconvenient because it's hard work. That's just how it is.

Stefan: On 19 January 2012 we launched a concept we'd been working on for years, and it all started along these lines: wouldn't it be cool if we could create a wristband that changes colour during the day, going from red to green as you 'charge' it with your own physical activity – whether it's playing a sport, going for a run or just climbing the stairs to your office?

Myself, Ricky Engelberg and BJ Naedele at Nike talked about it as a sweatband-like accessory and envisioned that the material itself would change its hues, like a chameleon, to register the energy you were adding to it by being active. We pictured the cotton sweatbands Björn Borg used to wear in the seventies – the kind that hasn't changed in fifty years, since before Nike existed, so we wanted to evolve it.

We created a mock-up design and a couple of 3D models without limiting ourselves to what was possible from an engineering and technology standpoint, because we knew some of the things we set out to do 'couldn't be done'. We decided to worry about that later, and just wanted to excite our leadership teams with the idea.

Mark Parker, our CEO, started at Nike as a designer. He has a very clear vision for what has true consumer relevance, and had always promoted the idea of colour as a simple performance measure. When we showed him our rough mock-ups, he looked at the models for about three seconds and said, 'How fast can you build this?'

With this immediate green light we set out to explore how to actually make it. The challenge was put to our lead designer Jamian Cobbet and head of engineering Aaron Weast. They sucked in their breath to this wild sweatband-like device with a massive flexible colour screen. Their reaction was, we'd love to, but it can't be done this way. These screens don't exist, and even if they did, to keep them lit would require you to run around with a car battery in a backpack.

I said, 'I know we can't replicate it exactly this way, so give it your best shot,' and challenged them to explore and investigate. After months of concept work, engineering validation and feasibility studies they delivered a handful of options for the team to review. One design in particular caught the team's attention. It was completely rounded and much thinner than originally imagined, but had an elegant, sleek look. When we brought the concepts back to Mark he pointed to his wrist and the yellow Livestrong band that Nike had created for the Lance Armstrong Foundation. Mark said:

> *'Can we flatten the top and bottom of the band so it fits like this one? Can we make it like a "smart" yellow band?'*

We took the feedback and worked with the teams to create what eventually became the Nike+ FuelBand.

It's a beautiful modern design that's durable, comfortable and designed for movement. Rather than the entire band changing colour, we focused on an elegant LCD display going from red through yellow, to green. The band is easy to use, but packed with innovative technology. We suspended the electronics on a flexible circuit board and enclosed them within a polymer casing, so it fits perfectly on your wrist, is water resistant and easy to wear.

We spent months developing curved batteries so they'd disappear within the shape, and made sure you have zero distraction when you move. And the band still delivers up to four days of activity on one single charge.

Ajaz: At the announcement in New York it was clear to everyone that Nike is launching a genre-defining, new category of product. People talk about 'wearable electronics' or 'social products' and 'the social economy', but here it is for real. A new device that's with you all the time, providing continuous, friendly motivation.

Stefan: We opened pre-orders that same afternoon, and sold out in sixty-seven minutes. But the reason we did was not just the product itself. It was the experience. The Nike Digital

Sport product, experience and tech teams worked incredibly hard to deliver a seamless chain of inspiration from the band to the app on the phone (via Bluetooth), to the web (through the built-in USB connector).

The entire experience is easy to use and creates a healthy addiction to reaching a daily goal you set yourself, by simply motivating you to get from red to green. We also introduced NikeFuel, a common metric that makes it easy for anyone being active to compare, compete and collaborate with friends, regardless of activity. And finally, we created a frictionless connection to your community through Facebook, Path and Foursquare.

Mark sums it up:

> 'This entire experience starts and ends with the consumer, it's Micro in that the FuelBand is personal, beautiful, simple and elegant, and at the same time Macro in that it's an incredibly rich social experience connected to everyone you care about through the phone and web services. It's a beautiful way to stay motivated to do more every day.'

The most amazing thing to me about this entire journey is that the final concept is true to the initial inspiration we mocked up, without limitations. In fact we improved on the concept so the launch product is better than what started life on the drawing board. Had we limited our initial thinking merely to what was possible at the time, it wouldn't have happened.

The automotive industry often creates stunning concept cars. But a few years later when the vehicle is put into production, some of the things that made it exciting or distinctive are removed because the more they show the concept design internally, the more they hear 'it can't be done'.

Ajaz: Talking about doing things the right way, the rigorous way, in product development or business process design, one of the biggest ways to go wrong, one of the biggest lures of convenience, is the bandwagon. For a lot of understandable reasons, it feels convenient to do what everybody else is doing.

Stefan: I guess, at a glance, some people might feel there's not so much difference between second mover and getting on a bandwagon. But there is a difference …

Ajaz: Second-mover advantage isn't about hanging on the coat-tails of the innovator. It's about knowing that winners can come second by refining and learning from what's already been done and then redoing it better. Bandwagoneering, on the other hand, means doing something just because others already have.

Had we limited our initial thinking merely to what was possible at the time, it wouldn't have happened.

Stefan: We've always had a candid dialogue, but don't you find it difficult dropping an inconvenient truth on a team you've only just met?

Ajaz: It's not painless but my job is to take the long-term view. That means making recommendations that will maximise the productivity of investments.

This truism was driven home a few years ago when Second Life – this online platform, this doppelgänger of real life – was all the rage. Everyone was going absolutely nuts for it, saying how virtual worlds were going to be the next big thing and, you know, one day when you can't tell the difference between the real and what we today consider 'virtual', they probably will be.

Anyway, during this frenzy for Second Life, we went to Italy to meet Fiat. Halfway through the presentation, the client said: 'What about Second Life? We really feel like we should be there. Besides, we mentioned it in the brief. Some agencies have even done designs of a virtual showroom, but you guys haven't addressed it.'

The room went quiet and I stood up. I went on to explain we believe and recommend there are more productive uses for their budget. Of all the agencies they had invited to pitch, we were the only one with the courage to tell them we didn't think Second Life was the right place to be at that time.

Now, we might have turned out to have been wrong. We weren't, but we might have been. But it would still have been important that we put it on the line like that, taking the long-term view, standing up for something more than the 'Next Big Fad'. As we said earlier, innovation by its nature has unknown outcomes but it helps you to become a better decision maker. Second Life wasn't the first virtual world we had seen. It was the most famous because it had captured the media's attention, but from what we could see, it still wasn't the right environment to make best use of the brand's resources.

Stefan: One of the drawbacks of convenience, oftentimes, is its falseness. An action that looks like the convenient one might very well not be. A diplomatic conversation with a client, with no confrontation or awkwardness or home truths, is convenient for your working relationship in one sense, but it could also stop you doing something great. It could be a kind of fool's gold.

It often feels convenient to follow conventional wisdom, for instance, about market research. You make assumptions, such as people want more choice rather than less. But it isn't always so. I've always loved the following story and the lesson is valid whether it's true or an industry myth.

Legend has it that when Sony was expanding their boombox line, they brought in a focus group of teenagers and asked them whether they'd prefer standard black or the option of various colours. The kids said how cool and exciting the new colours would be as they'd like to express themselves with them. Once the session was over, the researchers told the kids to pick up a boombox each – either in black or one of the funky new colours they had seen and endorsed previously – as a thank-you for their input. Apparently they all chose the black boombox. So, you have to pay attention to what it is that people do, rather than just what they say.

Ajaz: When Steve Jobs was twenty-nine, and the Mac was a year old, he used the comparison of a highly skilled, conscientious craftsman to explain Apple's thorough approach akin to an artisan ignoring market research but instead responding to his own inner need to build the best thing he can. The comment I always especially loved was this one:

> '*When you're a carpenter making a beautiful chest of drawers, you're not going to use a piece of plywood on the back, even though it faces the wall and nobody will ever see it. You'll know it's there, so you're going to use a beautiful piece of wood on the back.*'

Stefan: Talk about obsessing over details. We know Apple is truly unique, but what blows me away is how incredibly hard they work to stay ahead.

The word 'Convenience' isn't in their vocabulary, apart from making the world more straightforward for their customers. At a dinner last year when speaking about the immense efforts involved in preparations for their big announcements, I asked Greg Joswiak, Apple's VP of iPhone and iPod marketing, if they're able to relax after a big launch and he replied:

'We usually feel really good and congratulate ourselves for about a day. After that, it's right back to work on the next thing knowing that success is not an entitlement and we're only as good as our next product.'

Ajaz: I think in business and in life there are certain metaphors which 'say it all'. The Apple Store in New York is open 24/7, 365 days a year. That says everything about an organisation that's making its life inconvenient so it can help people whenever they need it. Ultimately both benefit.

Stefan: Most people are familiar with the acronym K-I-S-S, which stands for 'Keep it simple, stupid' …

Ajaz: As Leonardo da Vinci put it: 'Simplicity is the ultimate sophistication.'

Stefan: ... the term K-I-S-S was invented by Kelly Johnson, lead engineer at the Lockheed Skunk Works, which was the firm's advanced research department, where they created aircraft like the Lockheed U-2 and SR-71.

He ran Skunk Works to a fourteen-point management code that still inspires people today. But it's K-I-S-S that has always been the touchstone for me, especially since Wikipedia enlightened me as to how Kelly intended the term to be used. Let me read you a couple of paragraphs.

> *'While popular usage translates it as "Keep it simple, stupid",*
> *Johnson translated it as "Keep it simple stupid", and this*
> *reading is still used by many authors. There was no implicit*
> *meaning that an engineer was stupid; just the opposite.*
>
> *'The principle is best exemplified by the story of Johnson*
> *handing a team of design engineers a handful of tools, with*
> *the challenge that the jet aircraft they were designing must be*
> *repairable by an average mechanic in the field under combat*
> *conditions with only those tools. Hence, the "stupid" refers to*
> *the relationship between the way things break and the*
> *sophistication available to fix them.'*

Ajaz: That reminds me of Dieter Rams, a hero of mine. One of his Ten Principles of Good Design is that 'Good design makes a product understandable'. Another of his principles is 'Good design is as little design as possible'.

Our engineering team has a motto: 'Beautiful comes as standard.' Software code should be terse, elegant and efficient. It is like that bit of plywood behind the cabinet: something nobody but them ever sees. If you go above and beyond doing 'enough', you'll find the rewards – and I'm talking about personal satisfaction here, rather than money or medals – of your work will increase accordingly. The most rewarding projects in life always involve a bit of a struggle.

Stefan: Just because something's 'impossible' doesn't mean you shouldn't try it. Just because something seems a no-brainer doesn't mean you should do it.

Ajaz: Nothing in life worth having comes easily. If something seems to you to be too hard even to try, chances are that's exactly what makes it worth trying. Because switching services or ditching lame apps is so easy for a consumer, chances are you'll only produce work that stands out from the crowd if you make life a little difficult for yourself.

In William Dalrymple's book *From the Holy Mountain* he describes the ancient values of the Byzantine monks, but these could also be a synonym for keeping it simple, or any of the virtuous design approaches we've been discussing today:

'Balance, gentleness, absence of haste and clarity of spirit.'

'Good design makes a product understandable.'

Dieter Rams

Convenient is the enemy of right

Never have anything to apologise for.

Everything is in the execution

It might not be seen as sexy to roll up your shirt sleeves and get stuck into the details. But that's exactly where the action is. Being hands on is what makes the difference. If you lose sleep over things 99 per cent of your customers will never notice, you'll spot problems before even your harshest critic has time to do so.

Create structure to release and channel creativity

Never just go through the motions. Use process as a tool to give you the discipline to get things done, but don't expect to end up with a great product just because you've ticked certain boxes. Magic is the name we give to the friction between vision and reality. Strive for the impossible to deliver the amazing.

Make the complicated simple. And the simple interesting

Nothing in life worth having comes easy. Making life easier for people means making it tough for yourself. Doing something genuinely worthwhile takes imagination and commitment.

Discipline and focus. Focus and discipline

When efficiency or creativity are the highest priority, focus in solitude rather than meandering to the inevitable distractions and dilutions of interactions with others. It just gets in the way of getting stuff done.

0111001001100101

0111001101110000

0110010101100011

0111010000100000

0110100001110101

respect human nature

0110110101100001

0110111000100000

0110111001100001

0111010001110101

0111001001100101

Digital is the means, not the end. Technology sometimes obscures this ultimate truth, and makes it easy to forget that at the far side of an app, a Tweet, an anything, there's a person.

Make yourself proud by making people's lives easier, richer and more fun. Don't just give people choice, help them to choose.

Ajaz: Remember the movie *Big*, starring Tom Hanks, where he's a thirteen-year-old inside a grown-up's body?

Stefan: Of course.

Ajaz: Then I'm sure you'll remember the scene in the boardroom where an exec goes through detailed statistical analysis, competitive reviews, national research testing and concludes that their company should produce a building that turns into a robot as their next smash-hit toy.

All's going well until Tom Hanks' character, Josh, says bluntly, as any thirteen-year-old would, 'I don't get it.' The exec gets a bit flustered, tries to defend the concept – trots out all the consumer research, all the percentages they've got from focus groups – to prove it's a great idea.

Josh waits, listens, and then finally says: '… there's a million robots that turn into something. And this is a building that turns into a robot. So what's so fun about playing with a building? … Well, what's fun about that?'

Products, apps, campaigns launch every day that wouldn't pass the simple *'What's cool about that?'* question.

Stefan: When I see, say, a hot tub with a built-in web browser, my first response isn't usually 'Coool!' It's to scratch my head. Common sense is not always common practice, as they say. Just because something's new and different, doesn't necessarily mean it's better. Or that anyone cares. Now it's easier than ever to get caught up in your tech, and difficult to confidently predict what is going to strike a chord with people.

That's why, for me, the notion of 'respecting human nature' and behaviour only becomes more important as a touch-stone. It's about figuring out the problem you are going to solve and then using the technology as a tool to help.

Ajaz: In industry the word 'human' is often used in the abstract.

Stefan: Like 'human interface'. What's human about a mouse or a keyboard? We use them because they're better than what was there before. But they are not intuitive in the way speaking and touch is.

Ajaz: When the way to store a document is by clicking on the floppy disk icon, it doesn't seem right. There's at least a generation of people who have not used a floppy disk, but it's still the metaphor used. I feel the same way whenever I see the word 'Submit' at the bottom of a digital form. The word 'Submit' means, by one definition, to 'accept or yield to a superior force or to the authority or will of another person'. Is that what a company has in mind when they want someone to fill in a form? The word that should be used is 'Send' or 'Okay', not 'Submit'. Language is just as important as icons. So all this is hopefully just going to get replaced with something that's more natural, relevant and intelligent.

Stefan: We're at a time where voice recognition, visual recognition (such as face, objects, gestures, even mood), artificial intelligence and touch are converging to create far more natural interfaces with technology.

Ajaz: The expectation is that everything is going to be better, faster, smarter, cheaper and tailored to our needs. People reject the clutter and environmental cost of instruction manuals.

There are too many examples of products where they are redundant because the manufacturer made it so intuitive.

People expect highly considered design where steps have been removed and it's primitive to have to even wait for something battery-operated to charge. It should be ready and working out of the box. There is this expression 'plug and play'. Today, people don't want the 'plug' part. They want to get straight to play.

Stefan: In fact we expect new services to be smart, one step ahead of us. The standards are such that we need whoever designed it to have made sure that any friction in getting benefit from the product is removed. If not, we'll pick something else, even if it isn't the cheapest option.

Ajaz: The interface determines the interaction. So when a person discovers the best way for them to do a certain task is by using a particular app on their preferred device, it becomes indispensable. A good user experience results in a greater effect on decision-making than cost. People migrate towards the most convenient service for them because they have done the maths in their head and figured out the convenience, the time they get back, is worth more than making a small monetary saving.

Stefan: We have this principle in our group at Nike: 'Build it. Live It. Evolve it.' We always want to *feel* firsthand that things work as we were imagining. It's fascinating how different an experience manifests itself as it moves from theory to execution.

There is this expression 'plug and play'. People don't want the 'plug' part. They want to get straight to play.

Ajaz: People are attracted to what keeps its inherent promise. It's as true of products and service as it is of organisations that they seek careers with. 'I just think things should work properly' is how James Dyson, the brilliant entrepreneur, inventor and designer, describes what motivates him.

Stefan: It's about the organisation being a good editor-in-chief and curator to make life better for customers.

Ajaz: Help people to choose, don't just give them choice. Some researchers did an experiment in a supermarket in California. They set up a tasting booth. Sometimes they put six jars of jam on the table, sometimes they put out twenty-four different jars.

When there were more jars, more people stopped by to have a look at the table – like 60 per cent of passers-by. But only 3 per cent of them bought something, whereas, when there were only six jars to select from, 30 per cent bought at least one jar.

People were attracted to choice, but at the same time they were put off by it.

Stefan: In Sweden a few years ago they privatised the phone service. All of a sudden, overnight, Swedes went from having no choice of phone company to having a handful of options.

They had competing offers to evaluate and had to make decisions. Maybe they'd save money or have a more cust-omised service, but overall they weren't particularly ecstatic about the extra effort they had to make.

Ajaz: The unspoken irony behind the cult of choice is that you often have to waste more time and energy trying to get on top of all your choices than you save by making the 'wise' choice.

Stefan: Whether they admit it or not, people will usually thank you for taking the responsibility to curate their choices, for making things simpler for them, for doing the truly inconvenient stuff on their behalf. This means editing down product lines and ramping up product benefit.

Ajaz: The philosophy has to be: let's use the technology to make this the best way to do something, or let's not bother doing it at all. The goal has to be about making a new expe-rience an order of magnitude better than the existing way.

Stefan: eBay has grown its sales from mobile devices from $600 million in 2009 to $5 billion in 2011 partly because it's a more preferable, advantageous experience. Or take ordering a Domino's Pizza for home delivery. The mobile app can know where you are to save time with an address.

You choose the toppings and base from a list, so there is no ambiguity or mistakes made over the phone where you might get misheard. Domino's can instantly update any changes to the menu or special offers. Payments get automatically integrated into the company's systems. Once your order is placed you can track where it is. You can save orders and addresses so it's faster next time around. It becomes indispensable because it's the best way, so far invented, to get a pizza delivered to your door. One of the customer reviews of the app says: '100 per cent better than Internet or over the phone. Will never order any other way again.'

Ajaz: Food is a broad category with universal appeal: everyone needs to eat. With 'Jamie Oliver's 20 Minute Meals' and 'Jamie's Recipes' apps, the goal was to make it the easiest and most enjoyable way to cook.

Jamie is a pioneer. His passion for creativity and good food is at the heart of everything he and his team do. He has championed great food that's not complicated to make. He has democratised cooking for tens of millions of people by making it more inspiring, more interesting, more accessible and more fun.

At the launch of his '20 Minute Meals' app Jamie said:

'These days people are so busy and always on the go but they're rarely without their phones. When I set to work on this app, I wanted to make sure I gave people everything they would need to help them create great-tasting, home-made meals in around twenty minutes – that's less time than it would take to order and receive a take-out meal and yours will taste better.'

It's worth knowing the back story of the apps I worked on with Tristan Celder, Michael Maher and Ian Wharton from Zolmo, the software company we co-founded. I'd like to introduce Michael and Tristan to give a firsthand account.

Michael: If a company could capture *half* of the enthusiasm and commitment to perfection that we managed in those six months creating 'Jamie's 20 Minute Meals', they would find it difficult to fail. From concept to launch, every detail was considered and every eventuality planned for with passion and precision.

In many ways, the app market being so new and such an unknown was a fantastic strength. Every decision was made on gut feeling rather than on hard data, and in Tristan Ajaz had identified someone who possesses the rare combination of being both a visionary and a technical magician.

Together, over a blustery weekend in April 2009, we huddled around Ajaz's dining-room table putting together a vision that promised to 'reinvent cooking for the digital age'.

For me, recently returned from eight months' travelling, this was hitting the ground running, fuelled by Ajaz's endless energy and belief that anything is possible.

Jamie's team, led by Jamie himself, shared our vision and created the amazing '20 Minute Meals' concept – a masterstroke. Jamie's team had complete faith in us. This belief avoided decisions being made by committee, allowing us the freedom to deliver the complete vision.

Over the next six months it quickly became apparent that my role as project manager also included those of content manager, lead tester, producer, bookkeeper, tea maker, office manager, marketing manager and legal team.

Unavoidable in a start-up, the benefit of my multi-tasked role was that it enabled everyone else in the team to know exactly what was expected of them so they could focus on precisely what they were good at.

Tristan: Ajaz and I had previously worked together at AKQA. He was well aware I was interested in starting a business after our many conversations over the years, so I jumped at the chance when he called.

We then spent an evening at his house drawing up a business plan for Zolmo. That night I learned that an effective business plan doesn't have to be a hundred pages of expertly crafted prose. It just has to be fit for purpose, and in this case it was.

It was pretty clear we were missing a couple of roles. Fortunately, my friend of nearly twenty-five years, Michael, happened to be looking for a new challenge.

We both deliberated over whether two friends going into business together was a good idea before we got bored with the discussion and decided to go ahead anyway. Besides, it was a good fit, our abilities were polar opposites and therefore, together, were particularly complementary.

No one had really tackled the problem of creating a cooking app properly on the iPhone. The competition seemed to be looking to books to provide the template for what constituted a recipe app. Ingredients and method were displayed on a single scrollable screen, images were poorly shot and video was a luxury.

People weren't asking the right question. They were asking 'How can we bring the cooking book to the iPhone?' when they should have been asking 'How can we turn the iPhone into a tool for cooking?'

So that's what we did. Here was the chance to create an aid to cooking that was even better than books or TV. We didn't have the restriction of 'pages' like you do in a published book, or the linear 'one speed fits all' restriction of television. We could conceive a feature set that harnessed all the incredible features and context that a mobile device provides, but without burdening ourselves with the restrictions of legacy mediums.

We planned to create a unique step-by-step recipe interface, a photo illustrating each step, so that people could see they were on the right path, as well as a prompt for the ingredient required in that particular step. This was something that neither paper nor television was able to provide and made our offering unique. In addition to this we planned to include a shopping list that sorted ingredients by aisle as well as contextual videos that simplified techniques.

Michael: With Ajaz acting as, arguably, the most over-qualified quality assurance engineer in the history of digital, we made endless refinements to both the design and user flow, bouncing ideas between the core team.

On 30 September, having learned the hard way just how complicated it is to get recipes into a database, how expensive custom photography and video shoots can be, and, when it comes to a labour of love, that there is always more you would like to do, we submitted the app to Apple, hitting our target of delivery in September with three minutes to spare!

Tristan: Jamie Oliver's *20 Minute Meals* went on to gross seven figures and was awarded the Apple Design Award for 'outstanding design and innovation'. By asking the right questions, discarding our lack of experience and fighting through the obstacles that life inevitably deals, we had created something truly special. To this day *20 Minute Meals* remains the benchmark cooking app against which all others are judged.

We never let little things like 'not knowing how to do something' or an unexpected turn of events get in our way. We know that if we can will ourselves to face them, we'll be at an advantage. We embrace it and encourage it. Innovation is borne out of the unknown.

Ajaz: During that weekend in April, when we put together the vision and ideas for the app, we set a few goals. We wanted it to be the best cooking app on the planet; good enough that Apple would recognise it as iTunes App of the Week. We wanted it to be the highest-grossing app because that would prove people loved it. We wanted Jamie on the front of *Wired* magazine because he's a pioneer and we wanted his contribution to innovation to be celebrated. These four goals we set out right at the beginning. At our very first planning meeting!

The interface determines the interaction.
It results in a greater effect on decision-making than cost.

Stefan: Well, we did say there was no point in thinking small …

Ajaz: We achieved all the goals we set out to achieve and more. Although we already had a winning formula, about a year after we launched we changed everything again. We created a new app called 'Jamie's Recipes' which would be a free download and contain a variety of recipes to get you started but also give you a choice of recipe packs that could be purchased on demand, at low cost.

'Jamie's Recipes' would also be purpose-built and specific to the unique properties of the iPad, rather than trying to make the app designed for iPhone scale to a larger device. The number of downloads for 'Jamie's Recipes' was an order of magnitude greater than the previous app, so the risk the team took was worth it.

Stefan: It's an inspiring story. If, after our conversation today, I get home tonight and have a eureka moment, a new idea, I can easily search, and in fifteen minutes I'll have a level of understanding in a subject I previously knew nothing about.

Let's take building construction, for example. The conventional route is to use an architect and that's the way I started out when it came to designing a deck for my family's summerhouse in Sweden.

I knew what I wanted, but seemed to have trouble getting the architect I hired to articulate that into a design my family liked.

Each time he went back to the drawing board, it added another week to the project. I'm not an architect, but I'm curious and stubborn, so I searched online and found this free 3D modelling software, spent a few hours playing around with it to see what it could do, and then used it to build a virtual model of the deck my family wanted.

Then I took that to my amazing builder, Anders, and I didn't have to try to explain what I wanted – I just showed him. And he made it happen.

Ajaz: Think how much further we'll be able to take that by using 3D printing. It still sounds like sci-fi to most people, but affordable 3D printing machines that can make you solid, perfectly finished objects are here. They'll continue to become capable of bigger and more intricate printing. You could start a new business by recycling an old one.

Stefan: Before you start something new, you need to know it's a good idea.

Ajaz: I've never believed in sitting around and waiting for inspiration to strike. My mum says: 'There's a blessing in every good action,' which basically means 'go for it.' And I like Picasso's take on it: *'Inspiration does exist, but it has to find you working.'* Look hard at the world, and the best qualities within you, before you make something happen.

Stefan: 'Vibe' is the word you always use for those details that mean so much, right?

Ajaz: Yep, it's not about the content, it's about the vibe. The signals, the feelings. I have no idea where the numbers come from, or how you could prove them, come to think of it, but I've heard that when we're having a conversation, only 7 per cent of our communication comes from the content of what we're saying. Ninety-three per cent is non-verbal: body language and vocal tone.

Stefan: I'm sure that's why people started using smileys in email, text and IM. As cheesy as it is, it conveys an emotion that gets lost in plain text.

Ajaz: Whatever the breakdown is (and it almost certainly varies from case to case), it's clear that when someone or a brand communicates, he, she or it does so directly and indirectly at the same time. Direct communication you can call 'content' and indirect communication and connection you can call 'vibe'.

And the two insights here are: often it is vibe and not content that people respond to. And secondly it's possible (even easy) to focus so much on content that you forget to attend to your vibe, or you even screw up your vibe by becoming 'content-heavy'.

Stefan: Mae West said it in the thirties: 'It's not what I say, it's the way that I say it.'

She was talking, I suppose, about sex appeal, in a broad sense. One common denominator of products and brands that win is there's something about them that makes people say 'I want that' or 'I want to be part of that', 'I identify with that', 'I want to connect with that'.

Ajaz: It's about creating objects of desire. Weapons of mass seduction.

Stefan: So when you're creating something, you've got to pay attention to the vibe. Put the experience first and let tech be a smart enabler. Buying a 'smartphone' used to mean being smart, and patient. It meant spending an evening with the instruction manual trying to figure out how to get it to work, only to have to call a support desk in a remote country, being put on hold for twenty-two minutes, then being asked if the device had been plugged

It's not about the content. It's about the vibe.

into the wall! Now it means open the elegant packaging, connect, go.

I love watching my five-year-old son Lucas using my iPhone or iPad. He is so fluid it sometimes scares me. He knows where the App Store is, he knows he can only download free games, he figures out in fifteen seconds how they work (and if they're badly designed and don't work properly, his nine-year-old sister Melina deletes them immediately).

In his world, all this is created for him to have a great experience. Not for a company to show off. IT used to be synonymous with geeks who took pride in the fact that 'this is too advanced for you to understand'.

Now it's the ability to seamlessly invite customers into your world, let them explore, experience and create services that grow and become richer the more they engage with your brand.

Ajaz: The musician Brian Eno dismantles the idea of 'real' music versus music made using technology. A violin was 'technology' once upon a time, he says. In the UK, you know a new technology has become a normal part of life when you realise everybody in the country has intuitively agreed on a pet name for it. TV became 'telly', VCRs and tapes just got called 'videos', the ATM became the 'cash-point', the cellular phone became the 'mobile'.

Stefan: We also use technology to measure human feedback aiding, maintaining and enhancing a digital experience. The data gathered along the way is the single most valuable asset in the relationship between companies and their consumers. Not in some creepy snooping way, but in the sense of learning from and responding to what sticks and clicks with people.

Ajaz: If anything, IT should stand for 'Intuitive Technologies' and move from being an internal corporate function to a customer-facing asset. All focused around treating customer data as *the* essential resource.

Stefan: And treating it with care. A few years ago Michael Palmer wrote a great blog post where he compared data to crude oil: it's immensely valuable, but you have to refine it to use it, just as you can turn crude into products like gasoline or plastic.

Ajaz: The best organisations truly, deeply, understand their customers and figure out what to do next for them. A lot of insight can be found in whispers within social media channels. And in the digital data that we produce through our interactions with various services. So studying that data to extract meaning separates myth from reality.

Stefan: Facebook, Zynga, Google, Apple and Amazon are masters at analysing data, using it to refine a better customer experience.

I met with Zynga at their offices in San Francisco, and was pretty blown away by how closely they follow how their games are played. No wonder they've risen so quickly to become the world leader in social gaming.

At Zynga, every time a new feature is introduced, it's like mission control when NASA was launching a shuttle. The team watches in real time exactly how people are playing, where they spend time, and then continuously tweak the experience to perfect it and make it more addictive to satisfy the users.

Ajaz: There's nearly always an element of fear and loathing of anything new. It was the same when cell animation was replaced with computer-based animation. It has been especially true of digital games.

Stefan: Two hundred and thirty million monthly active players of its games. Fifty-five million daily users. The company had a market value of around $7 billion when trading started soon after its IPO.

But I guess the point is that all Zynga's clever use of technology is in the service of giving users more of what they want and responding to where they go.

They're an analytics company manifested as a gaming company. Instead of investing hugely in enough networks, servers and storage, they began leasing that entire infrastructure from data centres. That way they could quickly scale the size of their operation to fit players' behaviour. Customers, users, players, humans – whatever we want to call them, they were the ones dictating the size of the company at any given time.

Ajaz: Are you even a 'customer' when you're playing a game for free? Who knows? What I do know is that if you're forcing people to do something they are not inclined to do – call it 'made-up behaviour syndrome' – instead of enthusing them or making their lives more fulfilling, don't bother. Someone else will figure out a better way.

Stefan: Making people work harder than they're used to strikes me as a recipe for failure. I don't get 3D TV. If you want me to stick those glasses on, it ain't happening.

It's one thing to go to the cinema for some amazing, special 3D experience. But at home? No way. I have a hard enough time finding the remote control when I want it. I'm not going to go looking for glasses, too.

Naturally, the people behind the technology were totally gung-ho about it. But to my mind – and I could be wrong – it's like they were selling a car and calling it the most amazing thing ever except you have to wear a spacesuit in order to drive it.

I'm saying, hey, but I usually just wear jeans when I drive, and they're telling me, yeah, yeah, but check out this LCD heads-up windshield! Or whatever. It's inconvenient. It feels like it's going backwards because we did not need to wear special glasses to watch TV previously.

Ajaz: But people do usually embrace a degree of complication if it brings enough of a benefit.

This generation of 3D in theatres provides a solution to the cinema industry to help counter piracy and the digital home-entertainment boom. It was an economic solution that assumed a human need, a solution in search of a problem. If you spoke to the R&D experts at electronics firms who'd been looking into how people interacted with 3D for years, they always said it was an intense viewing experience that was best for bursts of gaming and other particular niches. Not a new standard.

It's an interim step because the home electronics industry needs to give people a reason to buy new TVs as we wait for the next-generation, organic light-emitting diode displays that produce deep black and stunning contrast. I think they look better than real life, but will cost less than previous-generation displays.

Stefan: I went to CES in Las Vegas, where all the new stuff gets rolled out. The show was obsessing over 3D TVs when everyone I asked at a personal level said the same thing: 'I ain't wearing those glasses.' Just the other day I saw a survey into consumer attitudes after the disappointing sales of 3D TV sets. The biggest complaints people have are price and those glasses, and only a minority express an interest in watching anything other than movies in 3D.

Ajaz: It's predicted that around two billion TVs will be connected to the web by 2014. This will result in more channels and services being available from the big screen in the living room. At that point, and especially with the 'lean-back' experience of TV, no one wants to learn to use a large complex remote control because most of them already have a non-intuitive layout with too many buttons. People also don't want the clutter of set-top boxes. The software and hardware in the TV should become sophisticated enough that these external units become redundant.

There should be a better experience of TV where it's more of a concierge, curating content and services around the viewer's needs. I'm looking forward to the day I can get

If you delight people, dazzle them with a flawless performance, you can put yourself in a category of one.

home, put my feet up, gesture or talk to a screen on the wall just as naturally as I am talking to you now. I want to be able to say: 'Show me all the goals that Arsenal scored at the weekend.' And I want them to appear immediately in the best resolution.

Then I want my TV to be smart enough to say something like: 'Here are the goals ... also, it's your sister's birthday. I can see she's online now, would you like me to call her back or arrange flowers?'

I want my TV or any of the other devices I use to work together in a more integrated way. And that's what's going to happen when the body of the device becomes independent from its mind.

So the 'mind' will be a digital concierge of data that knows all about me. It then transmits its intelligence to a 'body' or device that is context-relevant depending on my needs or what I'm doing at a particular time. Making it easy to move automatically from one device to another, whether I'm driving, walking up a hill or working at my desk. High-speed data networks like 4G and beyond will make it feel immediate and practical.

Stefan: If you remember the person in all this, if you centre the experience around people rather than the technology, a product will express itself in a more intuitive, more useful way.

Ajaz: More channels provide more opportunities to generate information. More information is only truly useful when companies can interpret it. Great retailers know all about the value of theatre in-store.

In *All Marketers Are Liars*, Seth Godin tells the story of his first visit to a Kiehl's cosmetics shop in Manhattan. It was no mere shop. It was a showroom, a shrine to these well-packaged, sweet-smelling toiletry items. He bought a pump of hand soap for $18. Afterwards, he realised he was paying about $6 for the soap and $12 for 'a souvenir of the shopping experience'. And he didn't mind!

Stefan: They make the case powerfully for some well-staged drama. But aren't we in danger of getting kind of analogue with this? It's still true that theatre captures people's imaginations, that it always has and always will. But shouldn't we bring the *Velocity* principles into this?

Ajaz: The Fat Duck, Heston Blumenthal's restaurant in Bray, has three Michelin stars and is therefore considered among the best in the world. People talk of it being a scientific approach to gastronomy. But for me, it's the art or theatre that surrounds the food, enhancing the entire experience.

The leather-bound menu with The Fat Duck logo intricately embossed on the outside and attentive typesetting on the inside is a thing of beauty. As is the uniquely detailed cutlery.

Everything feels absolutely considered to the finest degree, all in the name of giving you an unforgettable experience.

There's one course called 'Sound of the Sea' that comes with a soundtrack of crashing waves as diners eat, provided by an iPod nano enclosed in a shell. Heston Blumenthal did a series of tests with Charles Spence, head of the Crossmodal Research Laboratory at Oxford University, which studies how our brains manage to process the information from each of our different senses (such as smell, taste, sight, hearing and touch) to form rich, multisensory experiences.

The tests revealed that sound can really enhance the sense of taste. If you eat an oyster while listening to the sea, it tastes stronger and saltier than when it's eaten while listening to farmyard noises, for example.

The theatre turns The Fat Duck into a category of one. From a restaurant to a destination, from a dinner to a life experience.

This has been true for several years now; it seems impervious to the usual restaurant trends. The sheer finesse and accomplishment of its theatre is a big part of what gives it unique staying power.

In a time of endless choice and topics trending tremendously fast, if you delight people, dazzle them with a flawless performance, you can put yourself in a category of one.

Stefan: But it's a rare business that succeeds on theatre alone. Rarer than ever with the transparency that's omnipresent. Which means that in a lot of purchasing scenarios, one good reason is all we need to make a decision.

One particular endorsement, one particular product feature, one particularly resonant appeal to our identity or vanity.

In the animal kingdom, birds use various signals to attract mates, communicate fertility and so on. Theatre is the essence of these signals. The ones that are most highly prized, and most heavily relied upon, tend to be what's known as 'unfakeable signals' – the ones that cannot be feigned. If you've got it, you flaunt it. If you're not flaunting it, then you definitely haven't got it.

Ajaz: It's not about shaking your tailfeather shamelessly until everybody's staring. Make something people might truly want and make it in a way that makes you proud. Then let people know about it.

Stefan: And then let them let *you* know. Many companies still see customers who have something to say as an annoying obstacle to getting on with business. Which is crazy. Your most troublesome customers are potentially your most important.

Stew Leonard's weird and wild supermarket in Norwalk, Connecticut, has a sign on the wall when you walk in the front entrance:

> *'We believe that a customer who complains is our best friend because she cares enough to give us the opportunity to improve.'*

However you choose to do it, you've really got to obsess about making people's lives easier. And you've got to start not from the premise of 'what can we sell you?' but from 'how can we help you?'.

Ajaz: And actually meaning it.

Stefan: Right. Sometimes I think by removing friction and heightening our accessibility to each other, technology is allowing us, or maybe even forcing us, to become more human. The transparency that exists today means anybody saying one thing in your 'brand values' and doing another in your daily operations will get exposed sooner rather than later.

Which means businesses that can view things through a lens of humanity are more likely to be more successful. Human needs and desires, it seems to me, are more in charge than ever, more dominant than ever, more pronounced than ever. We find technologies that can serve and amplify them, and we're compelled to listen to them to prevent information overload.

So if you're asking 'How am I making someone's life better by what I'm doing?' then you've got the right idea. If you have to try too hard to change people's behaviour, you've got a tough row to hoe.

Ajaz: But if you take an accepted behaviour and improve on it, making it more accessible, or make an inconvenient behaviour unnecessary through better design, you've done a good turn.

Stefan: And you're not having to persuade people about anything. You're just showing them a better way. Technology can facilitate these timeless human characteristics in a more effective way.

Facebook didn't invent friendship, casual acquaintance-ship, awkward social situations, pointless chit-chat, self-promotion, drunken blabber, the joy of seeing family photos from far away.

It just took advantage of technology to blow all those things wide open in a new way.

Ajaz: Just by asking 'Wouldn't it be cool *if*?' or 'What's cool about that?' before bringing anything to market can take you a long way down that path. If the response you get is 'When can I get it?' you're probably on to something.

Stefan: The saying 'The more things change, the more they stay the same' still holds completely true for me. Over the years, I've found myself using it more and more, whenever I think we're getting too distracted from what we're here for by some shiny new tech craze. It's like Rebecka Törnqvist sings in 'Good Thing': *'Nothing has changed, but everything is different.'*

Respect human nature

Make yourself proud by making people's lives easier, richer and more fun. Don't just give people choice, help them to choose.

Understand people

It's not about the content, it's about the vibe. Velocity is about understanding people. Their behaviours, desires, motivations, passions and needs, and then applying technology in a way that helps them do it better. Velocity doesn't get blinded by technology. Human nature is its true north.

Make everything Useful, Usable, Delightful

These three words create the 'phenomena formula'. Because it's one thing to do work people can admire, but it's another thing to create something they will desire. Inspire your audience's emotions and senses by attending tirelessly to the details that enhance your impact. That's how you create experiences that are unforgettable and incomparable.

The interface is the brand

Digital touch points are fast becoming the most visible expression of any brand. It means every company needs to be a software company and that means learning to articulate your brand values through technology. Understand, experience and influence the entire customer experience at every touch point to ensure it's accessible and friction-free. Set new standards in quality, and excellence. Every touch counts.

Ask the right questions

'So what?', 'What's in it for me?', 'What's cool about that?' Make sure you have good answers because these are the three questions that will decide the fate of your work and the ones your customers will ask even if you never hear them. When your product is good enough, you should be delighted to answer them over and over.

~~M~~ ino ~~good~~

~~good~~

~~joke~~

~~survives a~~

survives a

~~committee~~ committee.

~~of~~ six.

For organisations with structures that sand down all rough edges and desiccate anything juicy, something terrible will happen: nothing. It's time for decision-making regimes that hold up to Velocity.

Have the balls to make the calls.

Ajaz: I'm not into 'groupthink' and there's a story I heard from the British political scene that demonstrates why.

Stefan: Perhaps we should avoid politics?

Ajaz: I usually try to, but this one's funny. And the politics are pretty much incidental.

Stefan: Okay, go for it.

Ajaz: A while back, when Tony Blair was Prime Minister, his wife, Cherie, was caught on mic saying something out of line about Gordon Brown, who at the time was Chancellor of the Exchequer, the man in control of the nation's money. Importantly for this story, the Prime Minister lives at Number 10 Downing Street and the Chancellor resides at Number 11. They're neighbours.

At any rate, Cherie's comments caused a kerfuffle in the press and it was clear that Tony Blair was going to have to say something, to address the issue somehow.

The occasion he chose was the speech scheduled at his final Labour Party conference in September 2006. The line he used to refer to Cherie's remarks, and to defuse the situation humorously, was 'Well, at least I don't have to worry about my wife running off with the bloke next door'.

It really did the trick. Everyone laughed, and it genuinely put the whole thing behind them. But here's the thing: Philip Collins, the speechwriter who wrote that joke, explained later that the sole reason it stayed in the script was because he'd only thought of it about fifteen minutes before Blair left for the auditorium. As he put it, no good joke ever survives a committee of six people, because there's always somebody who thinks it's not funny, or that it's too risky, or otherwise invents some reason – which might even be valid – why it shouldn't be told.

Take this story into a corporate context and substitute 'bold new product' for 'slightly risqué joke'. The situation is indistinguishable. And the company's ability to confidently 'tell the joke' (in other words, sign off on the product) comes down to judgement and intuition. More than that, it comes down to the willingness and ability of senior decision-makers to hear the judgement and intuition of one or two of their colleagues.

Stefan: Intuition has to be honed and calibrated to a particular case. And managers have to decide *whose* informed intuition to defer to in a particular situation.

To illustrate, there's the case of US Airways flight 1549. The one that took off from La Guardia at 3.24pm on 15 January 2009 and, five minutes later, landed in the Hudson, safely enough so that everyone on board survived and the few injuries that were sustained were minor.

What's so memorable about it now, for me, is what happened in the cockpit that day. It was actually the co-pilot who had been at the controls during takeoff and ascent when they ran into the flock of Canada geese and lost thrust in both engines.

When you listen to the cockpit recording of the whole incident, right after the bird strike, at the point they realise they're in trouble, something incredible happens. The captain says, simply, 'My aircraft.'

That's it. So succinct. 'My aircraft.' Which is shorthand for 'I'll take it from here'. There was absolutely no argument about it; literally four-tenths of a second later on the transcript, the first officer replies, 'Your aircraft.' Both the captain and co-pilot had decades of flying experience, but in that instant the fact that the captain had more hours logged on that model of Airbus counted in his favour, and both men in the cockpit knew it.

To continue the metaphor, you're never absolutely entitled to grab the controls. Well, I guess you are if you're captain.

But ideally, even as the anointed boss, you won't abuse that entitlement. If you're looking at it as just a hierarchy, as an org chart, then getting to make the call comes with having the job title. But, really, the true, innate ability to make a *great* call is something that's conferred on you, gradually, and it's also something you get the confidence to assert more as you gain experience.

Which is why using informed intuition is totally not the same thing as floating a blind guess. Rather, it's a calculation in which we bring our whole evolved and cultivated minds to bear on a subject.

Ajaz: Intuition complements better analysis. Machines beat grandmasters and win quiz shows. Achieving the goal of consensus from the team is very different from the goal of making the right decision.

The author Jim Collins, whose books include *Good to Great*, *Built to Last* and *How the Mighty Fall*, explains that 'consensus decisions' and 'intelligent decisions' are usually negatively correlated.

When his team studied where the best decisions come from and how the best decisions are made, as companies made a shift from good to great, they were struck by the absence of consensus.

Achieving the goal of consensus from the team is very different from the goal of making the right decision.

The research team learned that great organisations are environments characterised by incredible debate. Sometimes this would even mean people yelling and screaming at each other, so a very vigorous and engaged dialogue would emerge. The final decisions are rooted in discussion, supported with brutal facts. They are not authoritarian or domineering. Jim Collins puts the responsibility on every executive to debate and reach a point of understanding that enables the right decision to be made.

This usually happens before there is consensus agreement on what the decision should be. If everyone agrees too early on in the process then it usually means there has not been enough discussion and debate. It's about making the right decision rather than the most popular one.

Stefan: On my third day at Nike, as advertising manager for the Nordics, our marketing director Peter Zäll called me into a conference room at our offices in Solna, Sweden.

Nike had just finished shooting a campaign for our women's fitness products and there were seven boards mounted on the wall featuring athletes working out. Peter said to me: 'Two of these shots are perfect for this campaign; the other five suck. Which are they?' I was clutching for straws, using my vast forty-eight-hour Nike experience to figure it out. I gave it a shot and got one right. Peter then sat me down and gave me the extensive background as to why the two shots he selected embodied what we stood for as a brand, and ran me through the entire brand positioning.

This was the first of thousands of references I have gained over the past fifteen years from listening to Nike people. The sum total of all these references has helped hone my intuition to a point where today I am pretty comfortable not only picking out shots, but also evaluating business opportunities, designing solutions or positioning discussions. And most importantly, passing the experience on.

Nike is great at sharing this intuition across the organisation, and we rarely depend on outside research to evaluate our offer. The informed intuition is institutionalised through the people. We trust our gut.

Ajaz: It would be liberating and empowering for employees if more organisations could operate that way. The companies that I admire the most include Virgin, Nike, Apple, Google, Pixar, Audi, Ralph Lauren, McKinsey, Red Bull, J.Crew. These brands have a track record of excellence, conviction, a shared set of values. They also have the ability to democratise a dream but remain aspirational. They fight harder and don't cave in when they believe a decision is either the right or wrong thing to do. Many organisations aspire to emulate their ability to make the right decisions without second-guessing others or retreating to safe, familiar ground.

Stefan: Another astonishing feature of intuition is that, in order to function, it must actively *ignore* certain information and options that are on the table; good intuition doesn't get distracted from the essential truths. In fact, part of the art of intuition is in knowing what to ignore. In other words, 'don't let adverse facts stand in the way of a good decision'.

Ajaz: To be okay with purposely ignoring 'relevant' information? That's a tall order for your average management team.

Stefan: But other teams know better. Like in European football, where players got progressively taller and stronger over the years, and teams bought for height to keep up with their rivals – like a kind of arms' race but with legs.

There was one exception: the current Barcelona team. It's the shortest team in elite European football and the most successful. If you work out how to stop the other team having the ball, height comparisons are pretty meaningless.

The trust the coach put in the team's power to outplay 'conventional wisdom' has been rewarded with championships and Champions League wins. Now, they've reached such a superior level of football through that approach that other elite clubs are following their lead.

Ajaz: It reminds me of *Moneyball*, the true story by Michael Lewis that inspired the film starring Brad Pitt, about the Oakland Athletics baseball team's general manager, Billy Beane. The central premise is that the Oakland Athletics do not have the same resources or deep pockets as other teams in the same league.

A bit like the quote 'we have no money, so we have to think', Beane experiments with a radical approach where the collected wisdom of baseball insiders, players, managers, coaches and scouts over the past century is believed to be merely subjective and often flawed. The thinking that Beane pioneered had a big impact on the major league and in other disciplines.

Here's what Peter Bradshaw from the *Guardian* wrote about the film:

> '*Beane employs nerdy-brainiac Yale economist Peter Brand ... to apply a statistical, almost actuarial technique of recruiting undervalued players cheaply, on the basis of their hitherto unnoticed records, which would, combined, create an enhanced probability of success. It turns out to be a glorious triumph: a kind of blackjack-card-counting for baseball. But is it turning the sport he loves into a soulless game of number-crunching? It's an engaging, almost exotic film.*'

We have no money, so we have to think.

To create the exotic and engaging, sometimes you have to do something a bit crazy.

Stefan: Because it confirms that you 'have the balls to make the calls', so to speak. Tell me about a time you went crazy.

Ajaz: How about Christmas? The annual greetings card ritual. The in-house team assigned to that duty came up with an idea that was barmy, completely mad. It's part of my job to protect, nurture and, when they are ready, champion ideas. I signed it off *because* it was crazy. I said, 'This is so insane, we have to do it.'

Stefan: The microwave oven stunt?

Ajaz: We stacked forty-nine microwaves in a warehouse and set the timers to go off in sequence so they'd play 'Jingle Bells', with the 'ding' of each microwave serving as a note. Fortunately, it was a smash. Within days, it had been watched over a million times on YouTube. In music industry terms, that's platinum. On Christmas Day, the team got a great present when Kanye West posted one item on his blog – a link to that video.

Stefan: Maybe we should say a good joke doesn't survive a mediocre, or a typical, committee of six. Then again, a bad joke shouldn't survive a committee of *two*.

Nike has worked out how to make intuition an actionable corporate policy. We don't ignore facts. But we do allow the people and teams with the best judgement, belief in the opportunity, experience and vision in an area to be the arbiters of the data. We do this to fuel creativity for our product launches.

In 2002, when I was working on our World Cup campaign 'The Secret Tournament', we shot an epic film with twenty-four of the best players on earth competing in a three-on-three tournament on a tanker hidden from the world.

It was a big production and, as with any Nike film, the music played an enormous role in establishing the right emotional connection.

The music is usually the hardest part, because taste is so individual. Anyhow, after a number of failed tracks, we gathered in a small room at our editing studio in London and our agency played another new track they'd found.

After hearing the track, we had this funny feeling along the lines, 'this music absolutely shouldn't work, but there is something there …'.

'It almost sounds like *Elvis*,' said Phil McAveety, our European Marketing Director at the time.

'It *is* Elvis,' was the reply.

The track, *A Little Less Conversation*, had a great vibe but I felt it needed a more contemporary feel, so I asked if we could do a remix and add some depth.

It took heroic efforts by our business affairs guru, Mark Thomashow, the label and the Elvis estate, but in the end we got the master tracks from the vault in Memphis (in between the only two takes of the song you could actually hear Elvis chatting to the sound guys; it was pure magic).

We met up with a Dutch DJ called Tim Holkenborg, who went under the name JXL, in his Amsterdam studio, where he then gave the track exactly what it needed.

We still had to convince the Nike management team that an old Elvis track would be appropriate for a global football film by a youthful, future-focused sports brand in 2002.

I think it helped that we are Europeans, who knew what the tournament meant to people and loved the game, because after a few rounds of conversations that started 'Are you sure this is going to work?' and where we willingly laid our careers on the line, we were given the green light to go ahead.

After *that*, the rest was history: the track became a late addition to a new album of Elvis's thirty number one singles, and then became his thirty-first number one hit in more than twenty countries, which took him past the Beatles' record.

The platinum frame courtesy of Sony BMG is still on my office wall, as a permanent memento. It'll be in my office for as long as I am.

And the Nike campaign became a massive global success, helping to position Nike's football business to take over as the world's number one football brand.

Ajaz: There's a lot at stake in these decisions. There's a lot to spend if you greenlight them, a lot to lose if you don't trust your best people to do something new.

Stefan: So far we've spoken more about our instincts as individuals and leaders than about our people. That's an oversight we should address. If we mean it when we say we're devoted to flat management – and I am confident we do – we should say why.

Ajaz: For me the most important attribute a manager can have is the people they bring into the team, how they develop them and the standards of excellence they inspire. You're only a good leader *because* you have a team with which you can have frank, open-minded discussions that will enable you to reach the best decision. Maturing at what you do means learning to welcome constructive criticism, like you welcome anything that can make your work better.

Stefan: The trick is to get rid of oppressive status relationships without creating a noisy free-for-all. When you are unencumbered enough to move fluidly you need to use that freedom to push in the right direction.

In the Nike Digital Sport team we use filters as a mechanism to help us reach the right decisions. Filters are the collective wisdom of the team, made formal and written down. You might think this would be stifling or overly rigid, but, oddly, the opposite is true; it's liberating.

By writing things down in a checklist, you're free to forget about them for a few minutes at a time, long enough to come up with breakthrough ideas, but not long enough to go off course.

Here's what we ask ourselves:

1. Does it help athletes get better?
2. Does it have potential to add a million new members?
3. Can it be explained in two sentences or less?
4. Would we use it ourselves?
5. Is it simple, human and indispensable?

It's not that we will instantly reject anything that misses on one of these criteria, but we will be a lot less interested in developing it. And if we do choose to develop it, we'll know where it's weak to begin with, which makes a good brief and provides clear marching orders.

I don't understand when somebody from outside comes in to present an idea, or I'm talking with someone at a conference who's touting a business, and when I ask, 'So, would you use this yourself, this thing you're selling?' they respond, 'Well, you know, *I'm* not the target audience.'

What do you mean *you're* not the target audience? You should be! You should know more than anyone else about this stuff, and nobody should be more passionate about it. This doesn't mean geeking out to the extent that you lose the ability to translate it into a broad commercial opportunity and judge an idea's appeal to the non-obsessed, but it does mean standing up unequivocally for anything you develop and knowing how well it does what it's supposed to do.

Ajaz: That way, when you're all into something but equally all into making it fulfil its brief, you can be honest and critical without anybody taking it personally.

The 'filters' idea empowers people who would otherwise be excluded from certain processes. Like having ideas. It means creating a meritocracy that encourages ideas and contribution from every area of the company, not just 'the ideas people'.

In a world of subjectivity, filters smooth the way forward and depoliticise the decision-making process.

In that environment it's important to have a culture in which people are brutally honest with each other to not pursue ideas that will drain resources without having the necessary lasting impact. It's about being able to say no to ideas that are not compatible with the filters or where you want to be.

Stefan: In a world of subjectivity, filters are beautiful things. They smooth the way forward and depoliticise the evaluation and decision-making process. So instead of someone having to say, 'That concept's not right because of blah blah blah' (which even in the best circumstances and between the closest colleagues can come across as a rebuke), she can, for example, say, 'But would we use it ourselves?' And quickly, immediately, it becomes objectively clear – if not blindingly obvious – that, 'oh, yeah, well, I guess we probably wouldn't. Never mind. No hard feelings. Next!'

I think the clarity of your values, to which you've held steadfastly from the very beginning, and are all actionable, also serve as real filters.

Ajaz: Our belief is that good people do not like working for organisations whose values they mistrust but do enjoy being part of a team they believe in. We value our values. If a company can have a soul then our values are that. They help because they are real for us and provide a reminder of what we should be doing all day.

This is so
insane, we
have to do it.

They're not made-up, gee-we'd-like-to-be-this-way plati-tudes, which is all too often how it can work. For our team, our core, founding values of 'Innovation, Service, Quality, Thought' are consciously unflashy, reflect our passions and are our most important filter. They are an intrinsic part of our DNA and we're lucky we've never had to retrofit any inauthentic borrowed mission statements.

Author and branding guru Wally Olins tells a story about the time he was working for a big pharmaceuticals company. In front of the board of directors, he pulled out five cor-porate mission statements from five different drugs firms. He challenged the directors to pick their own firm's statement out of the batch. And they couldn't do it. Firstly, the mission statements all sounded pretty much the same. Secondly, their own 'official core values' had simply been out of sight, out of mind, for too long to be remembered easily.

Stefan: It's all too easy to believe.

Ajaz: One way or another, our values help us foster, every day, a company culture where decisions get made quickly.

Stefan: Collaboration is essential for any success, but some-one needs to know exactly what role each person, division or function will play. That's why any great sports team is coached by someone who knows how to draw the best out of every single player on the team.

Of course it helps having a superstar like Jordan or Ronaldo, but, at the end of the day, they can't do it by themselves. Engineers love to engineer. Designers love to design. And certain people keep it on track. We just have to make sure we don't use the forward as a goalie.

Ajaz: Somebody's got to be the one to take responsibility for seeing all those basic insights are always respected.

Stefan: And knowing when to say 'My aircraft'.

No good joke survives a committee of six

Have the balls to make the calls.

Give groupthink a rest

Debate, discuss, shout and scream, fight harder and don't cave in until you reach the right decision. Know that it's better to raise your head above the parapet with the risk of being shot down, than being a slave to the rules and never standing out from the crowd.

Filters are your friends

With a set of filters as your guide, you can steer a clear course to executing your project correctly, and avoid giving or taking offence as ideas are refined and rerouted by the development process.

Your project can only move as quickly as your team

Being a leader is less about playing by the rules than knowing when to change them. Filters free up the people in your team to discover strengths they didn't know they had, creating a Velocity-ready hunger for change and challenge to make the end result better. People resist change to their routine or challenge to their expertise for the usual reason: fear. Demonstrate how a culture of experimentation will benefit them, as well as your business.

Don't be a backseat driver, but do know when to take the wheel

Be a meritocratic boss, but still be a boss. Your team can only evolve and improve if you give them room to do the right thing by following their own instincts instead of always second-guessing yours. If you're not adding meaningful value, get out of the way. But when it comes to the crunch, you have to step up, take responsibility and say 'My aircraft' without a moment's hesitation.

HAVE A
PURPOSE
L>RGER THAN

yourself.

Velocity will disproportionately reward organisations and individuals that aim to make a meaningful and enduring contribution. Let your imagination and curiosity power progress.

Do the right thing: always play from your heart.

Stefan: I heard the chef José Andrés speak in LA a couple of years ago. José is an obsessive gastronomic innovator. Since he's been based in the States, he's been behind a whole bunch of clever and successful restaurants. But the story he told that really stuck with me wasn't about some revolutionary method of cooking. It was about the importance of imagination. This is what he said:

> *'Inspiration can come from anywhere. A while back, at home in Spain, I saw sunrays hit the ocean and got curious as to what sunshine would taste like. So I went about creating a dish that I thought tasted just like it. Now, if you ask a child what sunshine tastes like you'll get all sorts of answers, like vanilla, or lemon, or whatever they feel and think at that moment. When you ask an adult, they say: "That's impossible, sunlight doesn't have a taste." They've lost their imagination.'*

Creative leaders never lose their ability to dream. Their imagination, curiosity and passion have not taken the backseat in place of research, statistics and safe, standardised ways of thinking. Making your dent in the universe obviously needs goals, a plan and an incredibly robust process, but above all it needs a crystal-clear, bold vision. A vision is not just an idea. It's a transformational guide that everyone understands, and drives towards. And without rigorous process to deliver it, we've got nothing but talk.

Ajaz: The best leaders want to create something that outlasts them. This is different from ego-boosting personal ambition. That vision supplies the necessary drive and commitment to excellence to put mediocrity out of its misery. As a result, their organisations aspire to make a unique and distinct contribution to society.

Entrepreneurs are rarely happy with the way things are. The thrill of the chase of fixing what's wrong is part of the motivation. So it's easy for an entrepreneur to take the accomplishments of the previous generations for granted, considering a lot of accepted notions or methods to be prehistoric. Every one of us is influenced by ideas, environment and experiences, standing on the shoulders of giants. But it's because entrepreneurs think things are not good enough, cheap enough or fast enough that a lot of really great businesses are born.

Vision provides the necessary drive and commitment to excellence, putting mediocrity out of its misery.

The way they get there is through a higher level of commitment and discipline. Passion fuels an aspiration to be the best at what they do. Imagination keeps them thinking of what could be. They don't let anyone crush their spirit.

Business is also a way for entrepreneurs to express themselves to their fellow species. It is the consistency of a leader's values and behaviours that creates the culture of the organisation.

Like an athlete who won't give up, the organisations and people that characterise what we are talking about in *Velocity* have their fair share of difficulties. Everyone does. But the difference possessed by the champions we love is that they learn from when they're down and come back stronger. They are resilient. It's not convenient to be resilient, but it's right. It's the signature of excellence.

Stefan: By the time you reach adulthood, it's all too easy for your boldest and deepest desires to fade, and for you to just fall back on safe, standardised ways of thinking about life and work.

Picasso once said: *'Every child is an artist. The problem is how to remain an artist once he grows up.'*

Ajaz: When I was a kid, aged about ten, the headteacher asked me to illustrate the annual school magazine's sports section. Each sketch, whether a footballer, swimmer or basketball player, had one thing in common: there was a Nike swoosh in every drawing.

Stefan: So we were always destined to meet?

Ajaz: Yes. There must have been something in my subconscious even as far back as then. But it goes further. I got to work with Nike because we didn't get to work for another company. About twelve years ago we made a presentation to the director of a new Internet bank. We never heard from that bank again. But in a London taxi on his way back to the office, the director called his counterpart at Nike to let him know that he'd just been to see an agency worth meeting.

Stefan: Just like all the best adventure stories then, this book started with a good turn from an unlikely stranger.

Ajaz: Yes. We're talking about having a purpose larger than yourself and in a lot of companies people only talk about winning, losing or growth. We didn't win the pitch for the Internet bank, and as it happens they ended up not launching anyway. But we made the most sensible recommendations we could and clearly it made a strong impression. I learned it's not about winning or losing, but truly giving each occasion you invest time and resources in your best shot, because it creates other opportunities.

Stefan: The trick is channelling the endless curiosity of your inner child with the clear sense of purpose, outer direction and responsibility you have as an adult. Editing down all that amazement at the world into something you can act on, instead of just react to.

Ajaz: One technique or filter I heard Jeff Bezos mention to help him make a decision is what he calls 'the Regret Minimisation Framework'. In it you project out to being around eighty years old and you look back at your life and make commitments or decisions based on what you would have regretted doing or not doing.

Stefan: Speaking of something to act on, I saw this piece on Jack Dorsey (CEO of Square and co-founder of Twitter) on *TechCrunch* where he used the beauty of the Golden Gate Bridge in San Francisco as inspiration to his team for what he wanted his product to stand for:

> *'This is what I want to build. This is classy. This is inspiring.*
> *This is limitless. Every single aspect of this is gorgeous … So*
> *your homework this weekend is to cross this bridge, think*
> *about that, and also think about how we take those lessons*
> *into doing what we do, which is carry every single transaction*

in the world. We want to design the beautiful and build the impossible.'

This conversation is about aiming higher and having a purpose larger than yourself, and this is where we can learn from athletes. Great athletes often start with a childlike, impossible dream, then maximise their potential in a grown-up way: they train towards it.

Jesse Owens said before his record-breaking long jump at the 1936 Olympics, 'I decided I wasn't going to come down.'

Michael Johnson says you can never run the perfect race, but you can do something much more useful: *chase it.*

But you won't break records if you're not willing to get up on a pitch-black winter's morning to train in the rain. And you won't do anything at all if you just sit there. That's why the idea of the athlete we enshrine isn't just about the superstars, it's the athlete inside everyone.

It's not a way of pretending that we could all win an Olympic gold if we just wore the right shoes. It is a way of drawing attention to the potential for all of us to be athletes, if we so choose. It's about inspiring and giving yourself the best possible chance to succeed. Do you know what the word 'athlete' originally meant in ancient Greece? *'A contestant in the games.'*

'I decided I wasn't going to come down.'

Jesse Owens, before his record-breaking long jump at the 1936 Olympics

The core of why the athlete is such a useful idea, even if you can't get past the fifth push-up when you're in the gym, is that the athlete has to go through a series of stages that are remarkably similar to those that Velocity enables businesses to adopt.

An example: half the leading professional athletes today, if not more, started out in different positions, or in totally different sports, from the ones that made them famous.

Somewhere in their development, when they were already outstanding prospects, they had to face up to what they did well, and what they didn't, and accept that if they wanted to make the most of what they had they would have to change disciplines.

Reality – in the form of the body they rely on to excel – cannot be ignored in a day-to-day training plan.

Ajaz: Reality is also that somebody could beat you tomorrow, or your hamstring could go and ruin everything. That keeps athletes humble. Humility is when you're grounded and respectful to know there's always more to be learned.

Stefan: A sense of entitlement takes away the drive that's needed to succeed. When you are not improving the way you ought to be, or if you are getting injured when you shouldn't be, you have to be willing to rethink the way you do everything. And the body is there, like a tuning fork, to tell you, in record times or muscle twinges, whether you're on track.

Ajaz: On a Virgin Atlantic flight to San Francisco I managed to watch half of the excellent documentary *Senna*, about the legendary Brazilian Formula One racing driver. The plane landed before the film finished so I bought the other half on iTunes. You can't buy half a film, but you know what I mean.

I learned many things from that film. I learned that although sport should be and is often perceived as a pure form of competition, which operates by fair rules, it's not always the case. Politics gets in the way. I also learned about the amount of effort a genius like Ayrton Senna puts in even when the politics were not on his side. Envied by the bureaucrats but loved by the people because they responded to his courage, dedication and passion.

An athlete's training is about quality, not quantity. Athletes must find time for relaxation and recovery. They work hard and with focus, but they stop working, too – because you have to find the sweet spot between optimum performance and running your body into the ground.

Stefan: Right. Training for eight hours a day instead of three or four is equivalent to trying to instantly read every email, whenever it arrives and whatever time zone it's sent from. Clicking every headline every morning out of fear you might miss something is like spending all day watching the competition train instead of focusing on your goals. Velocity says our environment moves too fast and changes too often for us ever to delude ourselves into thinking we have complete mastery of it. Better instead to invest energy and time in making ourselves as responsive and reflexive, as fit and ready, as we can possibly be.

Ajaz: Tim Ferriss's idea of *The 4-Hour Work Week* is all about looking into yourself, instead of your BlackBerry, and making smart choices as to where you invest your time and energy. He talks about making yourself 'the ideal operating system for anyone who wants to operate in high-stress environments'.

That is what a professional athlete's training is all about. Don't pretend to control anything you can't but do control everything you can, and take responsibility.

Stefan: That's basically it. Today's elite athletes are a better example than ever of what this means because sheer talent is no longer enough to stay at the top. Another way they stay on top, but that many of us fail to emulate, is coaching. The rest of us go to school, maybe a degree, an induction, and that's it. Our official education is done.

Ajaz: I heard the extraordinary story of David Murdock, the eighty-seven-year-old billionaire, who has built a vast property portfolio and owns the world's largest producer of fresh fruit and vegetables. He dropped out of school because his teachers told him he was stupid.

Stefan: His *teachers* told him he was stupid. Imagine that. Not being encouraged by people whose job it is to further you.

Ajaz: David turned out to be dyslexic. After he left school he joined the US Army. There he came top of an aptitude test among a thousand other recruits. He now gives presentations at university campuses all over the USA sharing his story. He is providing the stimulation at schools that he didn't get. When students ask David how he managed to achieve his success he replies: 'I left school at fifteen years old and was told I was stupid so I have spent my lifetime learning.' He also said that he's worked harder than anyone else he knows.

Stefan: His resilience proved his teachers completely wrong.

Ajaz: David never got to develop a sense of entitlement. Today's athletes are the best at their sport – the fastest sprinters, the heaviest hitters – that the human race has ever seen. But guess what? Not one of them ever told their coach, 'Okay, I'm the finished article now. Thanks for everything – I'll give you a shout.' Of course not. They'll make sure they always have the best coach there is, from the first race to the last. To stay the distance, they know they have to keep learning and harness constructive criticism and new ideas from outside.

Stefan: Phil Knight, Nike's co-founder and chairman, reminds us what we're about. He simply says:

'Always remember the Athlete.'

It captures our reason for being in four words. Our co-founder, Bill Bowerman, showed the company time and time again how to draw insights from the world of sports to run a business. He preferred to be called a 'teacher' rather than a coach – he wanted to pass wisdom on to his students to empower them to achieve, rather than simply push or pull them to where he wanted them to go, like cattle.

Bowerman got incredible results too, with an amazing range of people. The process of making his athletes reach their potential involved scrutinising every practical detail of how they trained, rested and ate.

Mark Parker, Nike's CEO, has been at the company since 1979. He tells a story from his early days as a shoe designer when he had to present a new shoe design to the board of directors. He would talk a bit about the innovations and then unveil the new state-of-the-art shoe, but, no matter how great it looked or however many new features or fabrics it had, Bowerman would always do the same thing. He'd pull out his battered old-school scale and weigh the shoe:

> *'It's no lighter than the last one you presented. What's the point?'*

Bowerman was laser-focused on the same practical question that had set him about experimenting with his own running shoes in the first place: lighter running shoes mean faster times. What's the best way to make lighter running shoes?

Mark Parker has continued this legacy with the exact same clarity. He keeps reiterating that:

> *'We have limitless opportunities, but limited resources.'*

He is as clear as Bowerman and Knight about making hard choices, and always encourages the teams to 'edit to amplify'.

'It's no lighter than the last one you presented. What's the point?'

Bill Bowerman, Nike co-founder

His consumer focus is razor sharp:

'Help people choose by curating and making hard choices. We need to do fewer things better, and make sure our innovation agenda is built around true deep consumer value, not gimmicks.'

Ajaz: The best leaders create future leaders. They spot where the talents of an individual might be best suited and also act as teachers, developing people by conveying their skills to those around them and encouraging others to do the same.

I remember the first time I met you guys at a Nike conference room in Hilversum, Holland. Although it was me pitching, I got a clear sense of how strong your culture is, and how it permeates everything you do.

Stefan: It's by far what impressed me the most when joining the company in 1996, and I think there is so much to learn from this consumer focus. I've worked with Nike's VP of Brand and Categories, Trevor Edwards, for over fourteen years.

I remember going with him to a conference a few years back, and as the moderator summed up the day he asked the audience how they felt. The microphone was passed around and everyone politely said how great it had been. Trevor asked for the mic and I knew where this was going ...

He gave the most insightful, honest and critical assessment of all, as he felt the entire day had been wasted applying traditional thinking to the new digital playing field, instead of discussing the unprecedented opportunity to serve consumers.

After a brief uncomfortable silence heads started nodding and you saw the entire room rethink their day through a different light. And most of them probably realised that the most important learning of the day was his honest summary.

I asked Trevor to share his thoughts in this conversation:

Trevor: The single biggest opportunity today is that buying a product or service marks the beginning of the consumer relationship. Rather than the old 'awareness, interest, desire, action' model that relied on perpetual investments in marketing to draw consumers back over and over, we can now enrich almost any product or service and make it a meaningful experience. If a consumer wishes to share their information with us we can create individually tailored experiences. The more consumers interact with a company, the more value it can return. The 'logged in' state with a company is the most powerful way to build loyalty, and switch the energy from just telling people why something is great, to providing relevant products and services whenever, wherever, and however they choose.

For me retail has always been a great proxy for how well a brand connects. The first thing I do when arriving in a new city is spend a few hours checking out all sorts of stores, restaurants and malls. Observing how people react to products and services, seeing how product presentation and merchandising affects people's response, or when at a restaurant sensing how the balance between ambience, music, food and service contributes to a great, or not so great, experience.

I also always remember the first impressions when checking in to a hotel. If the check-in process isn't easy, everything else has to work really hard to make up for it. This is how I've always operated. I'm obsessed with understanding people's real needs. I like facts, statistics and research, but never let them take over common sense. I think it's the combination of having worked at a large metric driven company like Colgate, and the intuition-driven Nike culture that has given me the best of both worlds: facts and feeling.

But to come back to attention to detail for a second, as I think that without proper context this can be a distractor. It's actually attention to details. Every detail. You know you've succeeded when the consumer actually *feels* the passion and focus you've put into creating an experience.

Stefan: Belief in your ideas and an environment that encourages risk taking is incredibly important to create acceleration. I find it so unbelievably inspiring to see the seed of a wild idea grow to a world-wide phenomenon only because a handful of people were so confident, bullish and sometimes crazy to think that it could actually be done.

For example, after the Beijing Olympics in 2008 we wanted to use the unprecedented opportunity created by Nike+ to celebrate running across the world. The idea we pitched internally was called 'The Human Race', and we would invite a million people to run 10k on the same day. Every single runner that registered was to be given a red race shirt, and our aspiration was that, just as with the Chinese wall, you would be able to see this sea of red from the moon. Not many companies would sign off on this, but Nike did.

And 8 August 2008 was the day when the world ran. We had organised massive events in major cities all around the world, as well as a connected web experience that allowed anyone, regardless of where on the planet they ran, to log their run through nikeplus.com, and be a part of running history.

There has never,
ever, been so much
to play for.

Another one of these impossible Just Do It moments was observing the team that launched the yellow Livestrong band in support of the Lance Armstrong Foundation (LAF) fighting cancer. They pitched an idea where we would make six million yellow wristbands (one million for each of Lance's Tour De France wins at the time) and sell them for one dollar each. All profits would go to LAF. Almost everyone (including Lance) thought six million was incredibly ambitious, but the team were convinced it would work, and presented an incredibly ambitious plan including athletes and influencers participating in making the yellow band a must-have. Today over 70 million bands have been sold, and Nike has contributed $100 million to the foundation in the fight against cancer.

Ajaz: It captured the imagination. It also made giving to a cause you believe in accessible, and aspirational. It's all about engagement in the end. The week Nike launched those wristbands I bought several boxes of them for every AKQA office. We left a wristband and a letter from me explaining the cause on every employee's desk in the entire company. It meant so much to our team that the exact Livestrong yellow colour has become the permanent accent on the walls in our San Francisco office.

As our team has grown from a handful of people to over a thousand, one of our biggest challenges is to make sure we never lose the sense of community, ethics, trust and inter-connection that's been natural to our working ways and thinking from the start.

It means ensuring a purity of purpose, perhaps treating the company as if it is a product that can always be improved.

I sent these company-wide emails where I put a 'version' number for AKQA on them each year to show that we were making progress. In the entire first year of our existence I would say we were 'in beta'. I would point out any 'bugs' – things bugging me – so we could fix those in our next 'version'. It was also an opportunity to remove features that no one was using, that no longer made sense for where we wanted to be.

Stefan: We are lucky. Nike is a fresh and inspirational environment. There will always be an amazing new athlete and a great team. As we work with them, they help keep us fresh. We develop meaningful products and services by tapping into those athletes and we put a lot of passion into developing exacting products for them. And, in turn, our broader customer base, the billions of non-elite athletes, can benefit from those products and services, and feel an authentic relationship with the athletes where digital is the bonding tissue.

Ajaz: The brand becomes an operating system instead of a manufacturer.

Stefan: Exactly. An indispensable operating system is built on a platform. In our case that platform connects our consumers with us, as well as each other, and enables much deeper connections.

We now use data to give people personal, individual services and tap into forty years of athlete research.

We can provide much sharper product recommendations, as we know how people play, run, compete or train. And we can motivate you because we know what you like, and can serve content that matters to you. But we'll do all of this only if you allow us to, obviously.

Investing in a scalable enterprise consumer platform, so that you can truly service people's needs across digital and physical touch points, is the way to create a sustainable relationship with your consumer.

Ajaz: The author Richard Florida argues that the downturn that began in 2008 will be the third great economic 'reset' of the modern world – bigger than the 1870s or the 1930s, the two great depressions that changed everything.

Those two decades saw dramatic change, because hard times force speculators out of the economy and oblige everybody to go back to basics and figure out how to do things differently.

So with the development of dynamos, reliable electric generators of adequate capacity, you had the birth of the power grid in the 1870s. Then the huge changes in industry and expansion of roads and car ownership in the 1930s. Everything suddenly got so much faster, and that changed everything else in ways nobody could have imagined. Those who dared, won.

Stefan: Tom Clarke, Nike's former President, who has been instrumental in defining our team's charter, understands digital intuitively. When we were crafting our strategy, he brought a chart that tracked Nike Inc.'s revenue growth since going public in 1980.

There were three major growth spikes over those years, following the first entrepreneurial years. The first was going public; the second was the era of innovation with Nike Air and 'Air Jordan' – when history's greatest baller and the cutting edge of footwear technology came together to show how a sports brand could be much more; and the third that exploded the company beyond $20 billion in revenue was geographic and category expansion, when the company moved into new territories and aligned itself more clearly against sport categories.

He then pointed to today and said: 'We're on the verge of the next spike. And it's 100 per cent powered by digital.'

We stay relevant by expanding our connection and increasing our relevance to customers. On those terms, we are, without doubt, on the brink of a new era. A wildly inspiring era where smarter products and services seamlessly merge, connect people and create amazing experiences that make our lives better.

There has never, ever, been so much to play for.

Have a purpose larger than yourself

*Do the right thing: always play
from your heart.*

Be alive to being alive

Be driven by curiosity, not conformity. Young hearts run free. If you want to change the world, you have to shake off the security and routine of your grown-up way of doing things. It's not about 'big ideas' or 'small ideas', it's about good ideas.

Love is contagious

Seriously. If you're ashamed to say you love what you do, then, deep down, you don't. Do something you love, or find some way to love what you do. Put soul and humanity into your work. If you don't obsess over what you're doing, your customer won't either. If you do, and they do, the rewards will surpass your wildest expectations.

Open hearts first. Worry about wallets later

Your job is to serve, so the customer is always right, even when they're wrong. Sometimes they'll drive you crazy, but then so do your kids. If customers know you care and you keep proving it, you will keep your business thriving. Make recommendations that help your customer to achieve their goals.

Dream in widescreen, then push on in pixels

Dreaming big gets you enthused and is practical motivation – provided you break your dreams down into achievable realities and get going in meaningful ways. Heroes, and hero companies that you respect, can guide, teach and encourage you. Being good at being influenced is as worthwhile as being good at influencing.

In CONCLUSION ~

The most powerful force in the universe isn't technology.

It's imagination.

V

THE VELOCITY INDEX
Assess the Velocity of your business

In the Seven Laws of Velocity we have shared our thoughts on how to maximise your contribution in a world of unprecedented change and extraordinary opportunity. Visit velocitylaws.com for more ideas to help steer the future.

Acknowledgements

Stefan and Ajaz are appreciative of the contribution and support of everyone at Nike, AKQA, partners and friends. The people appearing within *Velocity* have been immensely helpful with suggestions, insights and encouragement. For that we are ever grateful.

It is said that a journey is best measured in friends and progress, rather than just distance. There are many people without whom our journeys wouldn't be what they are, so we also want to thank:

Susanna Abbott, Matt Bain, Tom Bedecarré, Wendy Chan, Nick Constantinou, Matty Corr, Luca de Meo, Steve Denning, Brendan DiBona, Georgos Dimopoulos, Tara Donovan, Duan Evans, Lester Feintuck, Bill Grabe, Mike Goldstein, Mike Greenlees, Jeremy Hildreth, Andy Hood, Kay Höök, Rei Inamoto, John Jackson, Louisa James, Simon Jefferson, Ben Jones, Sam Kelly, Anton Levy, Anne Lipsitz, Peter Lyle, Gino Mainolfi, Giles McCormack, Masaya Nakade, Dan Norris-Jones, Geoff Northcott, Jean Oelwang, Cathy Pittham-Wiley, Stéphanie Porter, Nigel Powell, Gail Rebuck, Neil Robinson, Erik Rogstad, David Rowan, Paul Sloane, Lars Stenberg, Michael Tchao, Matthew Treagus, Andy Tuffs, Nick Turner, Miles Unwin, Jason Warnes, Guy Wieynk.

About the authors

Ajaz Ahmed, AKQA

Ajaz is the Founder and Chairman of AKQA. He founded AKQA when he was twenty-one with the values of 'innovation', 'service', 'quality' and 'thought' to create an ideas company helping organisations embrace the digital revolution. Seventeen years later he is in the same job and AKQA has the same values. AKQA is the largest and most awarded company in its field with over a thousand employees worldwide. Ajaz works with leaders every day to formulate vision and new product ideas.

Stefan Olander, Nike Inc.

Stefan is the Vice President of Digital Sport for Nike. He oversees the company's global strategy for how digital technology will help athletes get better.

Over the past fifteen years Stefan has been a core contributor in evolving Nike's consumer connections across the globe through his roles in EMEA, Americas and currently at global headquarters in Beaverton.

From iconic brand communications to the creation of Nike+, Stefan has led teams that have redefined the industry and consistently delivered indispensable consumer experiences.

He is a native Swede with a Greek mother and resides in Portland with his wife and best friend Cathrine, and wonderful children Alex, Melina and Lucas.

Index

evolve immediately. entitle-
    ment kills 2, 5–45
execution 49–50, 53, 66,
    130–1, 144, 152, 208
experimenting 28, 29, 31,
    45, 79, 154, 195, 209,
    226

Facebook 14, 50–3, 56, 79,
    84, 101, 103, 113, 122,
    134, 170, 180
Facebook Effect, The
    (Kirkpatrick) 52
fad, next big 138
Fat Duck, The 176–7
feedback 18, 54, 60, 71, 94,
    101, 108, 133, 169
Ferriss, Tim 223
Fiat 105–9, 137
filters 201–4, 208–9, 218
Firemint 111
first-mover advantage 73
Flipboard 39–40
Florida, Richard 235
focus group 32, 50, 138–9,
    149
'forever tiny' companies 37
Foursquare 96, 134
free-roaming 112
friction, removing 26, 40, 59,

134, 144, 152, 179, 183
From the Holy Mountain
    (Dalrymple) 142

gaming 111–14
get going. Then get better
    2, 47–75
Gladwell, Malcolm 68, 69
Google 14, 86, 94, 100, 170,
    193
Greenberg, Alan 'Ace' 123,
    125, 126, 127

Harvey-Jones, John 73
have the balls to make the
    calls 3, 185–209
Heineken StarPlayer 109–10
HHCL 25–6
Hiaasen, Carl 34–5
Hilton, James 90–1, 93–4
human nature, respect 3,
    146–83
Hurley, Chad 100

imagination 3, 18, 54, 73,
    132, 145, 152, 176,
    211–39
innovation:
    is about embracing change
    61